In and Out of Every Season

William L. Hawkins

Parson's Porch Books

2018

Parson's Porch Books
www.parsonsporchbooks.com

In and Out of Every Season
ISBN: Softcover 978-1-951472-51-1
Copyright © 2018 by William L. Hawkins

All rights reserved. No part of this book may be reproduced or transmitted in any form or by any means, electronic or mechanical, including photocopying, recording, or by any information storage and retrieval system, without permission in writing from the publisher.

In and Out of Every Season

This book is dedicated to Lori, the greatest woman I've ever met and wife of 42 years,

and to our daughters
Abigail A. Hawkins, M.D. and Leah H. Bressler, M.D, M.P.H.

Contents

Introduction	9
This Blessed Burden 2 Timothy 1:3-14	11
Stand Up, Take Your Mat and Walk John 5:1-9; Acts 16:9-15	21
A Letter to My Father Job 19:23-27	29
Disestablished: **The Challenge of Congregational Life** John 15:12-17; 1 Peter 2:9-17	37
Living into Answers John 16:12-15	47
Praying Twice Exodus 15:20-21; Matthew 26:30; Ephesians 5:18-20	55
Mutual Encouragement in the Faith Psalm 133; Romans 1:8-15	63
Doing a "Beautiful Thing" Matthew 26:6-13; Ephesians 1:15-23	71
How to Love God and Honor Our Country 1 Kings 22:1-40; Romans 13:1-7	79
The Faith that Right Makes Might Matthew 7:12	87

Marriage Service: 97
Robert Bressler & Leah Hawkins

Marriage Service 103
Max Frumes & Abigail Hawkins

Memorial Service 107
Mark Raymond Krumnacher

Memorial Service 113
Jill Challender Shelley

Memorial Service 117
Donald Frank Selover

Memorial Service 122
Nancy Louise Hagy Chiles

Reckoning With Grief 126
  2 Samuel 18:24-33; Psalm 77:1-14

How to Help Others Handle Their Grief 134
  1 Kings 17:17-24; Luke 7:1-7

Introduction

These sermons address occasions you don't hear as much about because of their infrequence and in some cases their uniqueness. They neither addressed texts directly from the Revised Common Lectionary nor preached on high and holy days or seasons. All the same, pastors preach them as I say, *In and Out of Every Season*. As is true with all sermon volumes, it is a timepiece; in my case stretching over the last twenty years.

Here you will find sermons on occasions like weddings, an installation service, launching a building campaign, before a denominational body, introductory sermon before a new congregation, senior high Sunday, introducing a new hymnbook, dedication upon completion of a building program, memorial services, and matters relating thereto. They include sermons that attempt to address concerns and needs of a personal, pastoral and prophetic nature on civic, moral and political realities. Thus, they are both topical and *ad hoc;* some are more hortatory while others are more didactic in nature.

My gratitude is to the congregations I have served: Severn Presbyterian Church, Gloucester County, Virginia; First Presbyterian Church, Virginia Beach, Virginia; Graves Memorial Presbyterian Church, Clinton, NC, and First Presbyterian Church, New Bern, NC, where I've spent most of my time in ministry and continue to serve.

All proceeds from the sale of this book will go in support of the First Presbyterian Church, New Bern, NC, Bicentennial Fund.

My thanks is to my on-site editor and in honor of her memory, Nancy Chiles and to the Rev. Dr. David Russell Tullock of *Parson's Porch Books* whose invitation and encouragement to publish these sermons, has been an honor and pleasure.

This Blessed Burden

2 Timothy 1:3-14

In his autobiography *Life Work*, our nation's former poet laureate Donald Hall tells of visiting the British sculptor Henry Moore, who at the time was in his late 80's. Observing how even then, the aging artist performed his craft with painstaking delight, Hall was prompted to ask him what he believed to be the secret of life. Moore replied,

> *(t)he secret of life, is to have a task, something you devote your entire life to, something you bring everything to, every minute of the day for your whole life. The most important thing is – it must be something you cannot possibly do.*[1]

And with that, I welcome you, John Cherry McKinnon, to your chosen calling; or, more accurately, to the calling that has chosen you. The blessing in this calling is the promise of it being the secret of your life – a divine treasure, worthy of everything you will bring to it, every minute of every day, your whole life. The burden of this calling is its impossibility. You will discover and be reminded more often than you can imagine the limitations of being a clay pot, a mere earthen vessel.

Episcopal Priest Barbara Brown Taylor, captures this experience of both blessing and burden at her ordination. She writes:

> *Then [the Bishop] invited all the other priests to come up to*

---

[1] William R. Klein *Clothing for the Soul*, (Franklin: Providence House, 1996), p. 79.

the communion rail. As I knelt before the altar, I heard their vestments rustling behind me while the congregation sang a hymn...With my eyes closed and my heart hammering, I felt hands lighting on my head, my shoulders, and my back. At first their weight was comforting, like the weight of a winter quilt.... Then more hands piled on, and my neck began to hurt. I tried to straighten my back.... but it was too late.[2]

The gentle embrace of a *winter's quilt* paradoxically becomes a burdensome weight. I don't know if you experienced these contradictory sensations at your ordination last night, nonetheless, this blessed burden, John, is now yours.

First consider your blessings, *the rock from which you were hewn* (Isaiah 51:1). Consider those loved ones whose witness to the faith is in large measure responsible for bringing you to this point in your life. Some of those providentially, had their own life in the faith given shape here at First Presbyterian Church, New Bern. They are among the good ghosts awaiting you in this place. Paul's words to Timothy, model mine to you John, as I remind you of your grandmother Ida, your father Jim, and now you, John, who with Darci, have brought us Aidan, the fourth generation of McKinnons.

And gathered here today, are your many relatives who have lived the faith, that we are sure as Paul confidently tells Timothy, "lives in you." You have been traditioned in the faith; truly, the richest of life's blessings.

Other blessings are also yours, most recently your theological education. As you recall John, coming in between his

---

[2] Barbara Brown Taylor *Leaving Church*, (San Francisco: Harper San Francisco, 2006, p. 42.

transformation from chief prosecutor of Christians but before becoming a star witness for Christ, Paul tells the Church at Galatia, how he went away to Arabia for three years.[3] Thanks to archeological discoveries and advancements in linguistic studies, we know the word *Arabia* to be a code word for, *Richmond, Va.* There at the seminary you built upon the solid foundation of your past. And if Paul needed it even after his experience on Damascus Road, so does every would-be pastor.

For as another good ghost with connections to this place, that preacher of the Great Awakening Jonathan Edwards, said *there must be light in (your) understanding and fervency in (your) heart,*[4] you must desire your whole life long, this *light and heat*, head and heart, intellect and spirit.

The blessing of your formal education for ordained ministry, comes with a warning. Mine came in a backhanded sort of way, on the day of my ordination and installation three weeks and 26 years ago today. It came in a letter from a college classmate finishing law school, the place he believed I also belonged instead of seminary, seldom missing the opportunity to say so. His note was simply this:

> *Congratulations Bill:* You have just spent four years of your life studying dead languages, ancient manuscripts, and arcane theories about invisible things, and now you intend to get people to pay you to tell them what they should believe, become and do. Good luck!

---

[3] Galatians 1:17b-18a

[4] John E. Smith, ed. *Religious Affections* (1746), *Works of Jonathan Edwards*, Vol. 2 (New Haven: Yale University Press, 1959), p. 120.

It was warning enough about the dangers of the ivory tower! I heard it expressed early in my ministry, by an undertaker who said, *People don't care what you know, till they know you care.* I learned earlier still, when reading the historic principles of church government in the *Book of Order* where it says, *truth is in order to goodness.*[5] This is to say, something otherwise true even the gospel will seem less so if not altogether false, when the heart of the one proclaiming it, is not good. I believe I learned this best of all when I discovered that the great Calvin called his *Institutes of the Christian Religion* not a summary of theology, but a summary of *piety*, of spirituality; a life of servanthood and growth in personal holiness.

Already, your servanthood has been a blessing to many. You have shared the gospel in preaching and teaching, through leading worship, counseling and visiting, organizing and developing ministries and program events. Already, you and the gifts you possess have been affirmed through affectionate embrace, through sincere expressions of gratitude, through the delight in the face of some soul, who once lost, through your intercessions has been found. Not only are you blessed John, you need to know that you are a blessing, simply by being you. The hands that blessed you last night join those of this congregation eager to bless you onward.

These hands will however become heavy, a burden, draining. It is a marathon you've begun John not a sprint, so pace yourself. Drink deeply along the way, drink deeply from every blessed oasis in reach; for between them will lie lengthy stretches of desert, and your spirit will thirst all along the way. The disciples give voice to this burden. After failing to heal a boy of demon possession, they pleaded with Jesus, *Why could*

---

[5] *The Book of Order 2017-2019* F-3.0104, p. 12.

*we not cast it out?*⁶ (Mark 9:28) You will not be able either, John. You will not be able to repair the ruptured relationship that never should have ended in divorce. You will not be able stay the hand of the one who takes his life, rescue the teenager from the drunk driver and the tragic accident that awaits her, you will not be able to satisfactorily answer the countless questions that together form the stumbling block of our faith: *Why?*⁷ No longer an abstract philosophical question in the classroom, it has already become for you an answer requested by persons you know, by a family you love.

There is no education that can make you an expert on such matters, no insider information that magically creates an invulnerable faith. Your burden is to face honestly and openly the fact that our faith raises more questions than it answers, and to be willing to share with our members as they wrestle with the deepest issues of faith and life. To help people resist embracing counterfeit answers and destructive remedies, can drain your spirit, so be ready.

The intangible nature of encouraging youth in their spiritual formation, and of nurturing their parents' desire to love God, and grow in an ever-deepening love for God, will truly be an inspiration to your own faith. But just as often, your efforts will be met with yawning indifference, even suspicion. While you've been trained and called as a pastor in the church of Jesus Christ, you will be paid by how well you help run a religious institution, that like all institutions, is forced to measure itself

---

⁷ Paul Tillich, *The Eternal Now,* "Heal the Sick, Cast Out Demons" (New York: Chas Scribner's Sons, 1963). In this 1955 commencement sermon to the graduating class at Union Theological Seminary, he says *you will have to deal with this question* (the riddle of evil) *more often than any other* (pp. 60-61).

by numbers, and there is nothing intangible about that.[8]

Presbyterian Minister and novelist Frederick Buechner told the graduating class of our alma mater 30 years ago:

> *It is a crazy and foolish business to offer a service that most people most of the time think they need like a hole in the head. As long as there are bones to set and drains to unclog and children to tame and boredom to survive, we need doctors and plumbers and teachers and (entertainers); but when it comes to the business of Christ and his church, the service you offer appears to others as unreal and irrelevant, and at times will seem so, most especially, to you.*[9]

Encouraged by our cultural addiction to instant news, instant credit, instant coffee, and instant access, you will be tempted to join in with the short-cut gimmickry of offering instant spirituality. Form over content, method over substance, appearance over reality, is all the rage. And it is purveyed best of all by toothy-grinned TV preachers who always have the answers and who somehow manage to say just the right words that make people feel good. They have the numbers after all, so it must be sour grapes that have set our teeth on edge.

It will get to you! You'll wonder, who needs biblical preaching, and the time-tested theology and spirituality of the church catholic and historic, when you can swap it for the immediate cash value of: Peace-of-Mind-Possibility-Thinking-Da-Vinci-

---

[8] John Killinger, *Seven Things They Don't Teach You in Seminary* (New York: Crossroads, 2006), Chapter 1, pages 21-45.

[9] Frederick Buechner, *A Room Called Remember*, (San Francisco: HarperCollins, 1992), p. 142. I substituted the broader "entertainers" for Buechner's actual, *those who play the musical saw.*

Coded-Prayer-of-Jabez-Purposively-Driven-by-the-Gospel-of-Judas-and-the-Five-People-You-Most-Want-to-Meet-in-Heaven-Who-are-Spiritual-but-not-Religious?[10]

You will be burdened by people's fascination with the trendy and novel spiritualities here today and gone tomorrow. They will remind you of Abraham Lincoln's critique of Stephen Douglas's arguments for popular sovereignty. Said Lincoln: *they are as thin as the homeopathic soup made by boiling the shadow of a pigeon that had starved to death.*[11]

The burden is however, greater from within than without. Unless you are different than I am, you will be hearing voices that come from you know not where, *telling you that you will never be, never do, never have; ... this relentless chorus, never seems to tire of telling me how clumsy, lazy, weak, spoiled, thick-headed, (frightened), and doomed to failure I am.*[12] Lathered up before the morning mirror, too I often I see looking back at me in the words of Frederick Buechner, *at least eight parts, chicken, phony, slob.*[13]

Is it any wonder that Paul begins his letter by remembering Timothy's *tears*? Tears that strangely enough, prompt Paul's joy! Maybe the tears indicate for Paul that Timothy truly understands. And there is and will be much to weep about: your own doubts and fears, the weakness of your faith, your anger at God's interminable silence, the paralyzing sense of inadequacy.

---

[10] C. Clifton Black, *Where Do You Want to Eat*, Princeton Seminary Bulletin, No. 3, 2005, p. 300. I doubled his list.

[11] John Garvey, *Malnourished*, Commonweal, April 7, 2006, p. 23.

[12] Jon M. Walton, *Fed by Ravens*, Princeton Seminary Bulletin, No. 3, 2005, p. 308.

[13] Frederick Buechner, *Telling the Truth* (New York: Harper & Row, 1977), p. 7

But here is the thing, the truly crazy thing about it John: to endure all this to discover it blessing. The castor oil of humiliation, just the opening in you God is looking for. Perhaps. But without a doubt the paradox of this blessed burden comes full circle, at which time you will know yourself truly ordained. The very ill and melancholy cleric in George Bernanos' *Diary of a Country Priest*, cursed by seeing things as they really are, says of us and our kind: *We pay a heavy, very heavy price for the superhuman dignity of our calling. The ridiculous is always so near to the sublime.*[14]

Lest, those of you whose patience I've tested think this sermon is only about John and his ministry, you are mistaken. It is also your calling to *rekindle the gift of God*, given you. *The laying on of hands* of which Paul speaks, applies to that gift all Christians share, the gift given through the laying on of hands in our baptisms. John and I are not the only *fools for Christ*, (1 Corinthians 4:10; cf. 3:13) only *the servant of the servant of servants*[15] differing from you only in our avocation as pastors, sharing with you what is primary, our vocation as Christians.

I conclude with a challenge for every one of us, posed in Kierkegaard's parable about the church. It is a story about a large flock of geese, sequestered in a yard.

> *Every seventh day these geese parade to a corner of the yard, and their most eloquent orator gets up on the fence to speak on the wonders of geese. He tells of the exploits of the forefathers who*

---

[14] George Bernanos, *The Diary of a Country Priest* (New York: MacMillan Co, 1987), p. 74.

[15] David Steinmetz, *Memory & Mission* (Nashville: Abingdon Press, 1988), p. 68. The author states that the parish minister is, to use one of the titles associated by long tradition with the office of pope, the *servus servorum dei*, the servant of the servants of God."

dared to mount up on wings and fly all over the sky. He speaks of the mercy of the creator, who has given geese wings and the instinct to fly. This deeply impresses the geese who approvingly nod their heads. All this they do. One thing they do not do. They do not fly, for the corn is good and the barnyard is secure. [16]

Help us fly John, everyone, let us help each other, to fly.

---

[16] Ernest Campbell, *Locked in a Room with Open Doors* (Waco: Word, 1974), p. 174.

Stand Up, Take Your Mat and Walk
John 5:1-9; Acts 16:9-15

My Aunt Helen was not only a saintly woman, but one who possessed a marvelous sense of humor. When I was in middle school, she gave me a subscription to *MAD Magazine*. I've not seen one in years though I'm told it is still published. On the cover of each issue is found the cartoon sketch of the fictional character, Alfred E. Neuman, with freckles and a missing tooth. My favorite section was entitled, *Mad Magazine's Snappy Answers to Stupid Questions*.

I recall one scene where several women were standing inside the elevator on the bottom floor of the building with the doors still open. Outside looking in was another woman wondering about also entering the elevator. Right in front of her was an enormous sign saying, *Basement Floor*, and another, larger, fluorescent sign, lit-up in bright green saying, *This Elevator Going Up*. All the obvious indicators notwithstanding, she inquires of those inside, *Are you going up?* To which one of the women with a laconic smirk replies, *No, we are going to fool everyone and go sideways*.

You know why that slapstick cartoon comes to mind if you listened closely to the lesson from John's Gospel. Here is a man who had been lame for thirty-eight years. His useless legs had prevented him access to the very healing he desired. Tradition held that the Bethesda pool was miraculously transformed when mysteriously stirred by an infrequent, invisible, angelic visitor, as the controversial verse 4 explains. The stirring was believed to come because of the angel bathing, imparting to the water a residue of healing power available to the first infirmed person to follow into the water. The man's useless legs prevented him from reaching the pool as others rushed in before him.

For thirty-eight years he suffered this infirmity and John tells us that Jesus knew he had been at Bethesda a long time. Thus, the seemingly stupid question Jesus put to him, *Do you want to be healed?* You can almost hear his snappy answer to such a stupid question: *No, I've been here all these years just to enjoy the fun and frolics with this party crowd you see all around: the lame, paralyzed, deaf and blind.* Jesus' question could be interpreted as cruel. But in the questions Jesus puts to us, there is always more than the face value: *Do you want to be healed?*

Maybe healing isn't all it is cracked up to be? After thirty-eight years of waiting to be healed, the man may have become used to seeing opportunity after opportunity pass him by, and perhaps his only way of avoiding bitterness was to cease so urgently to want to be healed. Perhaps his attendance at the pool had become a matter of form. Where else was he going to be? After a while you adapt, and eventually organize your life around your circumstances. You make peace with things. One could even get accustomed to lounging around on a cool porch beneath one of the porticoes. Why risk losing a comfortable, shady spot in a failed attempt to be the first to reach the water? Very possibly he was able to live comfortably off his illness; nothing was expected of him, whatever he received was given and it had at the very least sustained him thirty-eight years. Health is nice, but if healed he would be expected to work, most likely out in the scorching heat. *Do you want to be healed?*

In theory of course, yes. But, and in a pinch, when we might gain it, many decide that the accustomed way of things will do after all.[17] Did you notice the evasive reply of the lame man to Jesus' question? It is neither a yes or no, but a typical human excuse which betrayed a sentiment that he no longer knew what he wanted.

---

[17] Arthur John Gossip, *The Interpreter's Bible, Vol. 8.* (Nashville: Abingdon, 1952), p. 541.

The paralysis of the body spread to become a paralysis of the spirit. The stupid question suddenly becomes one that is profoundly penetrating:

Do you want to be healed?

Spiritual and psychological paralysis takes many forms. The movie *The Shawshank Redemption*, is a grim story about life in prison. Escape and survival are the only items on the docket. But when the prison librarian is at last paroled his greatest longing had become his greatest fear: he is to be set free at last, and suddenly becomes terrified! For no longer are purpose and order provided him. He now must structure his life for himself and he is petrified by the prospect. We see him bagging groceries in a store where he is employed and then returns to his apartment alone. Though both his job and apartment were his last gift from the parole board, nothing else is predictable, and one evening in dark despair he hangs himself. He simply could not handle the responsibilities of his new-found freedom, and a life away from the only life he could remember. *Do you want to be healed?*

The recently liberated Israelites complained to Moses. In their selective memory they nostalgically yearn for the days when they were slaves in Egypt. Yearning to return to the misery they had just fled they cry out: *We remember the fish we used to eat in Egypt for nothing, the cucumbers, the melons, the leeks, the onions, and the garlic* (Numbers 11:5). *Do you want to be healed?*

How real is this conversation between the lame man and Jesus, and how accurately it speaks to the trappings of our humanity! Most of us know what is wrong with us. We know what is at stake when we have problems and set-backs. We know what needs to be done to make it right.

Ask any minister who counsels with people who have problems, and they will tell you what I'm going to say. And that is: most people have, by and large, already diagnosed their own problem. Many know the solution; they know the answer. Just as many realize however that living out the answer is a lot harder than simply knowing the answer. So, they come in search of a less threatening diagnosis and more importantly, for an easier remedy. But when you play the sounding board and hear them confirm to themselves what they already know, they prefer to return to business as usual. *Do you want to be healed?*

Matters are made worse when not individual, but a whole network of personal relationships conspire in preventing healing and wholeness to develop; when the illness of one has come to serve the sickness of the whole. When I was in college, the comedian Woody Allen was named "Theologian of the Year" by the *Wittenberg Door,* a journal that coincidentally has been described as the *MAD Magazine* of mainstream Protestantism. The article quoted several of Allen's stories that are not merely humorous but loaded with psychological and spiritual insight. One story is relevant to our topic. Woody Allen tells of a man who thinks he is a chicken. *Why doesn't your family take him to a psychiatrist, the friend responds. The brother replies, Because we cannot live without the eggs.*[18]

The psychoanalyst, Carl Jung once said to expect two results when giving people good advice: They almost always already know it, and they are not about to follow it. It is one of the constant and abiding ironies of human nature: all of us are too eager to settle for less than the good we know, even the best

---

[18] John Dart, *Woody Allen, Theologian, The Christian Century,* June 22-29, 1977, pp. 585-589.

to which God is calling us. Fear of the unknown and the comfort of the predictable stunts growth or keeps many locked in destructive habits or sick relationships.

The message of the Bethesda Pool can be heard from Paul in another reference, Romans 7, when in his bewilderment this great missionary of the church confesses: "I do not understand my own actions, *For I do not do what I want, but I do the very thing I hate* (Romans 7:15).

There are few things Sigmund Freud wrote not already anticipated by the Apostle Paul, even if this is overlooked by a secular culture which finds anyone who believes in God, lacking objectivity, narrow-minded, and exclusive of other views. Ours is an age that confuses the free exercise of natural urges and instincts as real freedom, and in so doing unwittingly pursue some other form of enslavement. *Do you want to be healed?*

Before us today are high school seniors, none of whom need healing that any of us are aware, have all the same, the need to grow, mature and develop. And growing is a way of healing, of *coming into one's own*. It is not the easy, painless transition you first assume it is to break free of parental oversight and the familiar and comfortable sights and sounds of home. Adolescent bravado eventually gives way to the discovery that it is a riskier matter of the spirit, mind and body than you imagine. On the other hand, not to go out on your own is a sort of paralysis that will stunt your growing into the persons God would have you become. Sometime during the dark days of the damp, winter cold, after the exhilarating novelty of college life wears off, when a permanent retreat to your warm, dry, cocoon in New Bern is most tempting. It may not be until then or some similar scenario when Jesus' words get your attention: *Do you want to grow up?*

The call to Christian discipleship is rejected not by people who are especially evil, or unloving, but by those attracted to mediocrity and succumb to the lure of the security of things as they are. Even the great Augustine struggled with the fact that the life to which he was accustomed before his conversion, held him more than the Christian life for which he really longed. And so, his sinful prayer is one we can all appreciate: *Make me holy Lord, . . . make me holy, but not yet!* [19]

And yet, this is in large measure why Christ was put to death, for we cannot stand someone who believes in us more than we are willing to believe in ourselves. I speak of the one who s our *beloved enemy*, the one the poet Francis Thompson calls, *The Hound of Heaven*, who is unwilling to let us settle for less. So, we must put repeatedly be about the task of putting the Risen Christ to death in our lives. It is as William Stringfellow once put it: *We kill the best man among us only after we have first killed the best man in us.*[20] *Do you want to be healed?*

Of course, you do, and so do I, all our appearances and actions to the contrary should not persuade us otherwise. Like Augustine and Lydia before him, like Brooks Bolton today, the mark of the Lord was placed on our heads at baptism. Not water from some pool supposedly bestowed intermittently with magical powers, but Christ himself is the source of our life, our healing, our coming into our own, our becoming fully alive, our realizing the image of God in our lives. In him is

---

[19] Saint Augustine, *Confessions*. Transl. R.S. Pine-Coffin (Baltimore: Penguin, 1961), p. 169.

[20] The source of this quotation is unknown, though I believe it may be found in the writings of William Stringfellow (1928-1985).

found the living water. With the name comes the promise, that if only in the life to come, certainly there our complete healing will be accomplished, and our lives completed. In the meantime, and to the extent we listen to our Lord's voice, we too will hear his question, but at the last his command: *Stand up, take your mat and walk.*

A Letter to My Father

Job 19:23-27

Dear Dad, this is a letter I knew I would write one day. Talking about anything of significance never seemed something we were good at, so had you read this before your death, I would expect the usual silence that came when I tried to discuss weighty matters. It is something I should have done anyway. For we both know that we cared greatly for each other, that you loved me, even as you knew how much I loved you. Early on I knew this unspoken awareness be-tween us would have to do. You'll have to forgive me for hoping for more.

The letter is being read in worship on All Saints Observance no less, the annual occasion when the church gives thanks for all those in our membership *who have died in the Lord*. I tell you this not because the church year or the church itself for that matter, meant much or anything to you. I say it because even though you were by all evidence indifferent toward God, I'm confident God was never indifferent toward you. If heaven should prove a place you are not welcome, I'm quite certain I will be turned away as well.

I once asked mom why you didn't have much to say to me, or any of us for that matter. She said it was because of the way you were brought up. Your own father spent very little time with you. The demands on fathers as breadwinners must have been severe and worrisome, especially for your father during the depression, and then for you, making it in the world of sales must have been hard and competitive. You had to be gone so much, missing ball games and school events. While Norman Mailer's *Death of Salesman* wasn't you, not by a long shot, and we were not his children not by a long shot either, something of that story could not help but resonate with ours. I don't know that I ever knew you at least in the way I thought I needed to.

You had a sense of humor, a great one at that. And you could entertain a crowd like few people I know. You kept your grandchildren enthralled with your antics. Yet I can only recall one time I saw you let loose and laugh, I mean, knee-slapping, chest-heaving, oxygen-depleting laughter.

I was 5 years old and you had just found me, hiding out from mom's wrath. She had come after me with a belt, after breaking a window with a football. As she charged out of the back door, I circled around to the driveway where the small opening under our porch led to haven: that amazing brick and concrete front porch, so roomy on the inside and always dark as pitch. I knew she wouldn't even try it. I didn't consider however, that you would soon be home from work and she would send you after me. Happily, my innocence proved disarming, for when you wiggled through that opening under the porch, I figured you were there for the same reason I was. Like you told mom afterwards between fits of laughter, wheezing out your story: *And then"* you told her, *out of the darkness Billy's little eyes appeared and with great concern in his voice said, Is she after you too?*

You showed little emotion otherwise. While you could be moody that was quite rare. I never recall a time you were despondent, angry or upset. The great Sphinx you were, the male Mona Lisa. Only time I saw you cry was at grandmother's funeral when I, a seminarian, participated in the service. Gathered around afterwards, you hugged me for a long time. I was the one who eventually broke your grip, such intimacy with you so unfamiliar or more than *I* could bear, or both. Interestingly, hugging became permissible after that.

I never knew just what it was that turned you off to the faith and the church. Perhaps it was the times. The last of the blue laws, Sunday closings, had fallen. I was only 6 then in 1960, but that is the year that began the downhill decline in worship attendance in our country following the post-World War II boom. Sociologists tell us that year marked the beginning of the end of church attendance as necessary for social acceptance and professional respectability. This becoming the spirit of the age, I assumed it to be the pretext you seized on to excuse yourself.

Clark had failed to do his work for Confirmation, along with three of his classmates. Remedial work was necessary, or they would not be eligible. Instead of backing the pastor who was right – *and you knew it* – along with the other three families, you took your leave. With mom as your mouthpiece the announcement was soon made: *You do not have to go to church anymore.* As George and Clark gave a sigh of relief, Mary Lynn and I looked the other way. Mom took me aside and assured me I would always have a sports coat and tie to wear since she knew how much I liked both Sunday School and Worship, willing to walk to and fro the five blocks from our house each Lord's Day.

Curious or intrigued, would have been a more apt description of my relationship with the church. Either way, Dad, you should have been a bit suspicious of me back then. Even the two correspondence courses, one for youth, the other for adults, I found in a Reader's Digest ad and nearly completed them both before discovering they were from the Seventh Day Adventists did not concern you – if you ever knew about them. When awarded the prize as star pupil at my Confirmation in that same Lutheran Church, well, that ought to have gotten your attention. So, Dad, I didn't become a minister because of

Bill Klein (Sr.), it was only because of him I am a Presbyterian rather than a Lutheran minister, providence smiling on me.

Yet, little did any of us know how odd I would turn out, for other reasons perhaps, but in this case, statistically; quite the exception that proves the rule. The rule according to Gallup and the Barna Group posted the same results: that if parents – especially fathers – do not attend worship with their children, their sons, less than 10% *ever* return. Well dad, the whirlwind you reaped is one you sowed: one son an atheist, one an agnostic, and one who is a minister. Here is proof that like you, God has a sense of humor, leaving me to *work on* my brothers; my brothers, who like you, I wouldn't trade for anyone else in the world.

I know I disappointed you and mom. I was the one you two had pinned your hopes, to follow in the footsteps of mom's father Judge Tom Henritze, and his father, same title and namesake. It didn't help that I was the one who looked most like the men on her side of the family, with the receding to disappearing hairline, so unlike yours and the rest of *our* family's hair, thicker and fluffier than cavemen. And different too was I from the rest in our household. I was at home in literature, the liberal arts and humanities; pre-law yes, but also, pre-ministry.

The one time in my life you seemed to have something serious to say to me, was your effort to talk me out of ministry. What can I say, but that in the sanctuary at morning worship at Second Presbyterian Church, Roanoke, Virginia in my Junior year of high school, I heard in Dr. Klein's sermon the *Truth*, I heard the Truth with a capital *T*, I heard the truth in a way I'd never imagined it. I'll not say more than that, but that was my calling – not to be a Christian, for that realization had already settled deep inside me, but to be a pastor.

I did so not to disappoint you, but because I could do no other, and trust me, there have been more times than I care to admit I would have outrun Jonah to escape. It took years, but you came around to it telling Mary Lynn what in your plan you intended to get back to me: *You ought to be proud of Billy.* Well dad, it worked! Thank you.

I don't think you ever saw it, but at the bottom of our church stationery, I've put a quotation from the 4th century Church Father, Gregory of Nyssa, whose fame in church history grew out of his insight and ability to articulate the distinctive place and role of the Holy Spirit in the Godhead; God's Triune nature. The quotation on the letter comes from my editorial rewrite and reads simply: *The only thing truly worthwhile, is to become God's Friend.* It is found in his paragraph that reads:

> *The only thing truly worthwhile, is to become God's Friend. This is true perfection: not to avoid a wicked life because like slaves we servilely fear punishment, nor to do good because we hope for rewards, as if cashing in on the virtuous life by some business-like arrangement. On the contrary, disregarding all those things for which we hope, and which have been reserved by promise, we regard falling from God's friendship as the only thing dreadful and we consider becoming God's friend the only thing worthy of honor and desire. This, as I have said, is the perfection of life.*[21]

It is this I believe with all my heart, soul, strength and mind, is the *Truth*. I don't know any words more profound or more

---

[21] Richard Foster and James Bryan Smith ed., *Devotional Classics* (San Francisco, HarperCollins, 1993, p. 157.

simple to put it. It names both the calling and adventure of faith. To become God's friend, includes becoming friends with God's people and then with all persons and creation itself.

Problem is, to become God's friend is difficult for you, perhaps for men born and nurtured as we all are in a frontier-spirited, pulled-up by your own boot-strapped mentality. For a person immersed in such a culture to desire such a relationship as *becoming God's friend* goes against the grain. You see I know men like you dad, men I like and admire. They are and have been in the churches I've served. Some of them belong to the church and some of those are daring enough to attend worship. But it is hard for them, I know it, and it is why so many of them are missing for so long, or for good. Something called *Muscular Christianity*, dreamed up over half a century ago to interest men by appealing to those *manly* qualities tried unsuccessfully to make a comeback in our day. It was doomed.[22]

I say that to become a friend of God requires an unmanly honesty, the honesty of owning up to the *truth* about yourself – the reality of your own vulnerability, utter dependency. It is to acknowledge something so humbling most people cannot bear it. Friendship with God opens one's eyes to life's uncertainty. To do so means allowing for ambiguity, of not-knowing, of not being in control. It will prompt your desire to trust the leading of the Spirit of Christ into all the truth, to proceed open-handed as the Spirit leads you. Like receiving manna, it must come fresh day by day.

These of course are all traits or wonderings the American male

---

[22] Stephen Prothero, *American Jesus: How the Son of God Became a National Icon* (New York: Farrar, Straus & Giroux, 2003), p. 101.

is taught to spend the first half of his life suppressing, denying, not allowing to believe even exists. Women are becoming good at this too, as their experiences in the professional world are of similar effect.

Then the moment of this great need comes when it can longer be denied. The misdirected pursuit of another wife, another job, another city, another hobby, all wears off in time. This is a need no substitute can ever fill, that which has been neglected so long at all costs presses in and at last comes due. To live in friendship with God is what we were all made for. Sometimes rumblings of this truth await retirement when you realize the disappointment of unfulfilled expectations, or the hollow feel of those you've achieved. Failing either of those, one's mortality can do it. I once told you this dad, how I would go and see these men in the hospital, some I'd never laid eyes on before, awaiting surgery. Lying there, waiting, fidgeting. It is serious, very serious. The prognosis offers little hope.

Yet they are in denial. There is always the hope that if you say it is not there and pretend it is not there it just may go away. Their bravado also protects their families, where ne'er a discouraging word of reality is admitted. I enter the room, to hear him say, *Hello Reverend why are you here? Betty asked me if I would come and see you. Aww! you didn't need to come and see me! I'll be O.K.* as he looks up at the IV drip. He talks about *getting out of here in 2-3 days*, though we both know he's not going anywhere, or anywhere that matters and that he is frightened.

I know he doesn't want me to pray with him as much as he wants me to do so more than anything else in the world. He fears if I do so he will cry, and with good reason. If he cried he would appear to be as he is – as we all are – weak, humble, dependent, vulnerable…the fertile soil from which sprouts a relationship with God. Because, when people break down, some break open, giving God's Spirit a place of entry. And if a relationship begins, a derivative benefit is as the apostle put it: *when I am weak then I become strong* (2 Corinthians 12:10).

I was not there at your end, none of us were, but I take my consolation in this, that when your heart stopped beating God's heart was the first to break for all of us, who loved you. Including me, who loved you as completely as I knew how, without ever beginning to understand you, or you me. That is O.K.: everything in its time. And it is your time now, for that relationship you missed out on in this life, I pray is at last fully yours.

Disestablished: The Challenge of Congregational Life

John 15:12-17; 1 Peter 2:9-17

Though our U.S. Constitution was produced by a congress consisting mostly of Christians, the first clause of the First Amendment prohibits the establishment of an official religion. The apparent irony goes deeper when we acknowledge the contributions of Christians in the formation of our government, beginning with the revolutionary war itself. This was something particularly true of Presbyterians. Historian Lefferts Loetscher said that the fires of the American Revolution were fanned from Presbyterian pulpits such that the British described it as the *Presbyterian Rebellion*. When King George III asked what the trouble was in the American colonies a member of Parliament replied, *our colonial cousins had run off with a Presbyterian parson.*[23]

The organizing pastor of First Presbyterian Church New Bern, NC, John Knox Witherspoon, was the grandson and namesake of the only clergyman to sign the Declaration of Independence. *I'm required to say that!*

Whatever you may think of the disestablishment clause, the biblical wisdom and Reformed theological stamp that shaped our Constitution is unmistakable. The principal author, James Madison, was educated at Presbyterian Princeton where he was a student of John Witherspoon. Remembered as *The Father of the United States Constitution*, Madison helped produce what

---

[23] Lefferts Loetscher, *A Brief History of the Presbyterians,* 3rd edition (Philadelphia: The Westminster Press, 1978, pp. 73- 76.

Lutheran historian Martin Marty has called *a thoroughly Calvinist document*. Marty claims that the Constitution supplies the checks and balances any Presbyterian would love, for the unspoken implication found throughout, is the conviction that while humans have a great capability, self-interest would always turn them against the common good if left to themselves.[24]

Madison believed that human beings, religious or not, should not be trusted on their own. It was held that this healthy suspicion would serve the greater good of those very persons and in turn, the lives of those people they would be entrusted to govern. Madison learned from Witherspoon what the Bible had taught concerning human nature nearly one-hundred and fifty years before Lord Acton was inspired to make his famous quip: *Power corrupts, and absolute power corrupts, absolutely.*

Madison and his co-authors had observed how this power placed in the service of religious intolerance, had lit the flames of incessant wars throughout Europe in the preceding centuries.[25] They knew how when conflicts arise, human nature takes over as each side deputizes God as their heavenly mascot, wearing their religious halo in the transparent attempt to cover the will to power. As American Christians we have cause to be grateful for the way biblical wisdom is distilled in our Constitution, particularly that first clause of the First Amendment.

---

[24] Dean K. Thompson, *Celebrating Our Presbyterian Heritage: John Witherspoon, James Madison and the U.S. Constitution*, The Presbyterian Outlook, July 4, 1991.

[25] Richard B. Morris, *Seven Who Shaped Our Destiny: The Founding Fathers as Revolutionaries*, (New York: Harper & Row, 1973). Madison said that this separation (religion and state) formed, *the great barrier against usurpations on the rights of conscience. So long as it is respected and no longer, these will be safe. Every provision for them short of this principle, will be found to leave crevices at least through which bigotry may introduce persecution; a monster, that feeding and thriving on its own venom, gradually swells to a size and strength overwhelming all laws divine and human,* p. 206.

While early on the disestablishment clause served to prevent our nation choosing one Christian *brand* or denomination over another, it could not prevent our national conscience to assume Christianity to be, however unofficially, *the established* religion. So, it was essentially for nearly two hundred years, our Jewish friends were looked upon as a tolerated though benighted minority.

Challenges to this assumption were to come from brand new religions, spawned upon American soil: the Unitarians and Mormons in the 19th and Jehovah's Witnesses in the 20th centuries.[26] However unanticipated, these challenges were bound to multiply and accelerate with the passage of the Naturalization and Immigration Act of 1965.[27]

With national quotas lifted, immigrants of the so-named *Fifth Wave* came to our shores in numbers as never before; not only from Europe and Mexico, but in the hundreds of thousands from Asia and the Orient. Introduced into our tax-paying citizenry have come Muslims, Buddhists, Sikhs, Hindus, and followers of other religions. Where have they settled? San Francisco, Chicago, Atlanta, New York, and – Chapel Hill no doubt! – these are some of the places you might expect. But when the December 2002 issue of *Our State Magazine* featured an article on a Buddhist Temple outside the Brunswick County town of Bolivia, North Carolina, well, it got my attention.[28]

---

[26] Franklin Littell, *From State Church to Pluralism: A Protestant Interpretation of Religion in American History*, New York: Macmillan, 1971.

[27] Diana Eck, *A New Religious America: How a "Christian Country" Has Become the World's Most Religiously Diverse Nation*, San Francisco: HarperCollins, 2001, pp. 6-7.

[28] David LaVere, *The Road to Enlightenment: In an Unexpected Corner of North Carolina, Followers of the Buddha Live Gently, Practice Charity, And Make Big Plans for the Future, Our State Magazine*. December 2002, pp. 68-71.

Though Christians in the United States will continue to significantly outnumber adherents of other religions for the foreseeable future, the landscape of religious life in America will never be the same. No longer is the net effect of the disestablishment clause which prevents one brand of Christianity lording over the others. It now takes the form of not showing preference for the very religion of Christianity over any other. The ground under our feet has shifted, caused not so much by the popular target of atheism and secularism, as by a more expansive religious pluralism. It has changed much that we as American Christians have for too long taken for granted, beginning with our privileged status. Some ten years after the passage of the First Amendment, when in 1802 President Thomas Jefferson coined the slang phrase *Separation of Church and State*, he surely misspoke. Were he alive today, he would have stayed closer to the Constitutional wording of, *Separation of Religion and State*.

The First Amendment squabbles being debated in the courts today come because of our nation's evolving religious pluralism. These divisions, I know, go on not merely among us but inside each of us. When it comes to *intelligent design* my heart is with the Bible enthusiasts, but my head is with the Constitution and the methods of scientific inquiry. Like any of you, I am troubled by the impersonal materialistic assumptions easily presupposed when discussing evolutionary biological processes like mutation and natural selection. Yet, "intelligent design" is not particularly biblical, and only raises the larger question, of whose intelligent design? The deistic god of Newtonian physics? Marduk and Tiamat of the *Enuma Elish*? Uranus and Gaia of the Greek Poet, Hesiod? Or is it the design resulting from the work of the Hindu Trinity of Brahma,

Vishnu and Shiva? – to name only a few intelligent designers.

When it comes to prayer in public schools, my heart and head are likewise split. We know prayer as a means of grace opening us to the movement of God's Spirit, reviving God's image within us, and equipping us to ever more grow in the likeness of Christ. There is nothing like the intimacy God makes real to you and me in prayer. But when classmates and teachers can be of another religion or none whatsoever as protected by the Constitution, any compromise praying to a generic *Higher Power*, only disgraces the relationship of sincere devotees of different faiths and violates the constitutional rights of those of no faith.

My heart and head are similarly divided when it comes to posting the commandments in government buildings or displaying them in monuments on public grounds, when done to the exclusion of any other commemorative or historical markers. The role of the Ten Commandments in western jurisprudence is unquestioned, and any revisionist history that suggests otherwise needs to be challenged. But when religious groups surprise us with claims that the commandments are not religious per se, then tie their witness to several thousand monuments erected half a century ago as a publicity scheme of Paramount Studios to hawk Cecille B. Demille's 1956 Hollywood production, I'm left to wonder what faith is being witnessed.[29]

My friends, I submit to you, these First Amendment battles are the wrong places in government and society to witness our

---

[29] Frank Rich, *The God Racket, From Demille to DeLay*, New York Times, March 27, 2005. Paramount Studios accomplished this project in collaboration with the Fraternal Order of Eagles, a nationwide association of civic minded clubs found by theater owners.

faithfulness to Christ. The efforts of our denomination and those ecumenical and interfaith alliances to which we belong on state, national, and global levels, have and continue to offer faithful attempts to witness to the gospel in the public sector, controversial and troublesome as they may be at times. But these realities are not my concerns today, nor do I imagine for any of us as pastors or elders of congregations.

It was 1960, five years before the landmark Naturalization and Immigration Act, cited by historians as the year marking the end of Western Christendom (beginning with the conversion of Constantine in 321). The symbolic date was timed with the elimination of the *Blue Laws* in the United States. It was the last legally protected protestant convention to fall, born of the efforts of the moral reformers of the 19th century to combat the three social sins: drinking, gambling, and Sabbath (or more accurately, Lord's Day) breaking.

Pressures for this change came not from atheists or adherents of other religions, but from the commercial and business interests of Christians just like you and me. Buoyed up by emerging wealth and increased recreational opportunities, other places to go and other things to do became more attractive than participation in the life of a local congregation. Worship on the Lord's Day became an interruption. With the pretense of church commitment no longer necessary for social respectability, many of us became nostalgic for more of that pretense.

For those of us ordained as elders or pastors 25 years or so ago, it was old news when in the late 1980's Robert Lynn reported to the Lilly Foundation on the increasing challenges and pressures to congregational life. There once was an *ecology*, he called it, of such things as public, essentially *Protestant* education, the Sunday Schools, youth programs, conference centers, publications, mission societies, that together formerly aided the congregation in Christian acculturation of her members. Many are gone and those few that still exist, he said, are but a shadow of what they once were.[30]

All this is to say, what every elder and pastor knows or needs to – working at congregational life may never have been more demanding than it is today, and perhaps never more important. I don't know when simply showing up has mattered so much. We who have been nurtured in the church that we've by now also loved and served for years have always known that the congregation is where the action is. Now it is the only place, and perhaps this is best. As nothing can be taken for granted, we realize nothing ever should have been. Faith formation and spiritual development to form the peculiar people we are called to be is again our proper task.[31]

No one can do it as well as our congregations, yours and mine, trusting the Spirit of God to lead us along the way. It is in and through congregational life where we affirm the Supremacy of Christ's Lordship. We do this by embodying his humble servanthood in our witness to and sometimes sharing with, those of other faiths and of no faith. It is in congregational life that we explore the depth of the affirmation, *I believe in God the Father, Almighty, maker of heaven and earth,* who is at one with the Divine Logos and the Spirit that both broods over and gives

---

[30] T. Hartley Hall, IV, *Back to the Future: The Pastor as Resident Theologian*, *AS I SEE IT TODAY*, A Publication of Union Theological Seminary in Virginia, Spring, 1994.

[31] Clifton Kirkpatrick, *Wake-Up Call to the Presbyterian Church (U.S.A.), Statistically, we are not losing people to other churches. Our problem is that we are losing our people to the secular world – to no active church affiliation. All of us – pastors, elders, and deacons – need to give special attention to nurturing our members.*

life to all. Our faith provides that wider and broader perspective to the instrumentality of science – both its theories and findings. It is in congregational life where we experience personal and corporate prayer opening us to the love of God and neighbor unknown and unavailable in any other way. It is in congregational life where the keeping of the commandments is found at the center of a constellation of practices and disciplines that shape Christian conscience and form us as the aliens and exiles the New Testament says we are, prodding us to *honor everyone and love the family of believers.*

The intrinsic worth of congregational life, like a sleeping giant, which rises now and again, to wow a nation. While traditional disaster-response organizations have been faulted for acting slowly following the Gulf Coast hurricanes, the churches and her agencies knew immediately what to do and how to do it right the first time with congregations of every stripe: welcoming, housing, clothing and feeding thousands of victims.[32]

No technology, no pleasures no activities or opportunities that are now or will ever come available, can replace or supersede the priceless experience of a Christian congregation, worshipping, living, studying, praying and serving together. There is no greater good that can be accomplished, no better work that we as pastors and elders can be about, than our labor of love to build-up the church *Christ gave himself up for*, and against which *the gates of hell shall not prevail.* (Ephesians 5:25b; Matthew 16:18)

There is never a better time for you and me to be Christian

---

[32] PCUSA.NEWS@HALAK. PCUSA.ORG. "After Katrina, church agencies out-quicked government, secular groups."

than right now, otherwise the Lord would not have put us here! *You did not choose me, but I chose you* (John 15:16a) said the Lord Jesus. Friends, let us claim our chosen*ness* by building up the community of faith, seeking to do so in the love and humility, courage and fortitude of Christ himself.

Living into Answers
John 16:12-15

Legendary preacher of the first half of the twentieth century, Harry Emerson Fosdick, tells the following story of his childhood. As a little boy, he observed that whenever the branches of the trees swayed, he felt the wind in his face, and saw its effects on the landscape. He concluded that the swaying trees caused the wind to blow. When he learned later that he had reversed cause and effect he was glad for having kept his previous conclusions to himself. But as he continued to mature he took a more enlightened view of his former naiveté, becoming thankful for once holding to his mistaken belief. However wrong, it answered his curiosity for a time, till the full truth was revealed.

I consider Fosdick's experience a parable of faith and life. From world history to our personal histories, we are always living into answers. How many of our present-day conclusions and solutions will one day be viewed as primitive or backwards by future generations? Centuries ago, humankind believed the answer to the ordering of the universe was that the sun and all the planets revolved around the earth. Though mistaken, we humans managed to get by despite our ignorance, just as those my age and older got by before today's technological marvels. How often we've met the incredulous stares of our children, who with their computer mastery and cell phone wizardry, are utterly amazed that we manage to eke out our survival, living as we do on a minimum of today's dizzying array of wireless electronic gadgets. With faxing, e-mailing, tweeting, facebooking, texting, instagramming, snap-chatting etc., at the greatest of distances we communicate as if the other is in the next room.

None the wiser about what we presently do not know, we who are living at the outset of the 21st century continue as those before. And as always, we benefit from the utility of numerous things we do not understand. From the laws of the universe to the intricacies of quantum physics; from a GPS directional system in the comfort of your own car, to commercial-free satellite radio – like gravity itself – we enjoy the benefits of nature and human ingenuity, while the overwhelming majority of us have little or no clue about how much of it works!

The point I wish to make is that every generation, ours included lives with little choice but to trust and depend on countless preliminary answers, while the full truth or complete realization of latent potentialities in the created order and human inventiveness, lay in the future. Human knowledge is limited and fragmentary: no human answer is true for all time, at least not true in the same way. We make do with things as they are, while we look with confidence toward the future. It is this faith in progress that is claimed to be the *real* faith of Americans, if not the entire western world.

Theologians claim that religious or not, modern people have shoved aside trust in divine providence in favor of a human-engineered salvation. That is, we are building our own Towers of Babel up to the heavens. To be sure, Europe and America are more secular than the other four-fifths of the world's population. The risk is that in the absence of humility and gratitude to God, our great knowledge will become demonic, turn and destroy us. Then again, faith in progress and faith in providence make for a close parallel.

Scientists pursue discoveries that will lead to inventions that will eradicate disease or enhance human life. We believe the answers *are* out there and *in* here waiting to be discovered. And as Christians, we pray and work to see that such discoveries will benefit the other half of the world that lives on average at less than $2 per day. If we didn't hold this belief, no effort would be made to find cures for diseases or remedies to problems, political, economic and social. While not faith in God, this expectation is analogous to it; believing what is not seen.

The same holds true of our life in and with God. Although there are no stages of Christian perfection, our calling is to a life-long quest to grow in the likeness of Christ. In ways uniquely personal, our lives are intended to be an ever-unfolding experience of becoming Christ-like. It is an experience the Bible tells us, that while personal it occurs only as it is both personal and communal. None of us was meant to go it alone. Despite feeling that following Christ is a continual starting over, there is progress, growth.

We live by faith and hope of this future. The Apostle Paul says, though we, *now ... know in part, we shall then understand fully* (1 Corinthians 13:12 RSV); that we are to be confident that *though our outer nature is wearing away our inner nature is being renewed day by day* (2 Corinthians 4:16). He also said that as we are *working out our own salvation with fear and trembling* (Philippians 2:12), we are simultaneously *being transformed into the same image* of the Lord, *from one degree of glory to another* (2 Corinthians 3:18).

The night before his death, our Lord gathered with the disciples. It was his purpose to prepare them for his death and what would be ahead for them. Having followed Jesus at great risk to their own lives he now says of all things, *it is to your advantage that I go away* (John 16:27). Jesus was telling them the future held much more and were he to stay and things to continue their growth in faith and life would cease.

Understandably, they were quite puzzled. He explained, that what he had taught them and that they had not understood in his presence, would become increasingly clear, in his absence.

This is God's plan: The Spirit of Truth will come and bring to their remembrance all he said and did. Better still, the Spirit will continue to explore or develop more fully the deeper truth of his life and words for all of Jesus' followers, present and future. About this unknown future however, this much we do know: The Spirit's leading us into all the truth, will be consistent with all Jesus said and did. By the power of God's Spirit, we are to live into answers that our endlessly creating Father God revealed in the earthly life of God's Son, thereby fulfilling the Triune God's plan since before all time.

All this new truth cannot be borne at once. Sin, ignorance, conditioned responses to life as usual – human nature being what it is – means that we will receive or accept this new truth, gradually. To the frustration of the prophet and visionary, it seems Jesus' followers move to the Spirit's guidance at glacial speed. That is why so many of them are usually dead, often having been put to death, before their wisdom is embraced by their former persecutors. God's answers do not come easy nor are they readily accepted. As Reinhold Niebuhr once put it, *The old (order) does not give way to the new without (first) trying to overcome it.*[33]

And yet, not all change is genuine growth. Being led into all the truth requires patience to *test the spirits* (1 John 4:1) to see if they are of the Lord.

---

[33] Reinhold Niebuhr, *Leaves from the Notebook of a Tamed Cynic* (New York: Da Capo Press, 1976), p. 102.

It staggers the mind from our vantage point in history, to read the defense of slavery once preached from southern pulpits in the mid-nineteenth century. Though this *peculiar institution* was assumed in the New Testament and received Christian support for nearly 2,000 more years, during that same expanse of time Christian concerns over this great evil mounted. The Spirit led readers of the gospels to more fully comprehend the way Jesus related to all persons, and that the Apostle Paul's words: *There is no longer Jew nor Greek, slave nor free, ... male nor female; for all ... are one in Christ Jesus* (Galatians 3:28), to be words that were eternally true, while his comment: *slaves, obey your masters*, (Ephesians 6:5; Colossians 3:22) a particular ethical command given the realities of that day and in the mistaken expectation of Christ's imminent return and *not* an endorsement of slavery. It has taken nearly 2,000 years to be able to say that out loud to a congregation and receive the genuine approval of everyone present.

Similarly, the role of women in society and the church provides another example. The full equality of women is still a goal, efforts towards which are recent in the history of humankind – a phenomenon largely still exclusive to the industrialized nations of the west. Acceptance of women in leadership positions represents only a minority among the world's Christians. But many churches, including the Presbyterian Church, have come to believe Jesus' egalitarian view of the genders is testified to by his example. And we believe his example to be God's expression of his intention as found in the creation stories of the Old Testament, and that gender hierarchy is the latter construct of fallen human nature, and every effort to maintain it is regressive, and in opposition to God's original intention at creation.

Perhaps the most divisive is the least understood – the

acceptance of the gay lifestyle can be a legitimate Christian lifestyle. Scriptural condemnations in the Old Testament have to do with the failure "to be fruitful and multiply." In the New Testament what is being condemned is the same gender rape of conquered peoples and elsewhere prohibited as a liturgical act in the worship of idols in some aboriginal religions. Monogamous relationships are not considered as a possibility, but only that homosexual love is always promiscuous and only taken up by bored and adventurous heterosexuals.

As the late Presbyterian Minister, William Sloane Coffin, former chaplain of Yale University and Senior Pastor of Riverside Church, New York City has written:

> *For Christians the norm is Christ's love. If people can show tenderness and constancy in caring that honors Christ's love, what matters their sexual orientation? Shouldn't a relationship be judged by its inner worth than by its outer appearance? When has a monopoly on durable life-warming love been held by legally wed heterosexuals?*
>
> *What did most to help my ("homophobia"), more than an accumulation and analysis of the evidence available, was to spend time with gay people. Familiarity bred only respect, never contempt.*[34]

And what can we say of how the Spirit will lead us through what the lost prominence of the church in western culture. Has our coziness with the established order, politically and socially, served to mute the voice of God, and is God now using this marginalizing to re-establish us as the *resident aliens* (Acts 7:6)

---

[34] William Sloane Coffin, *A Passion for the Possible: A Message to U.S. Churches* (Louisville: Westminster/John Knox Press, 1993), pp. 65, 67.

the New Testament says we were meant to be? How will the Spirit lead the churches through present debates about human sexuality, or the unforeseen array of choices now available through advances in the medical and physical sciences, coming at a pace so rapid that they have out-stripped ethical reflection?

Where will the Spirit of truth, the Spirit of Jesus Christ who is one with the Father, and who is *the same yesterday, today and forever* (Hebrews 13:8), lead us in these and other matters? We have many things yet to hear says Jesus that the Spirit of truth has to say. We go forward in confidence that the Spirit of truth will lead us into those answers.

This why I believe the adventure of the Christian faith is so exciting. As I've told Confirmation students for years now: there is nothing else in life that compares to living as a Christian. For like life itself, a vibrant, living, active faith in Christ is not a *closed shop*, defended by fearful vigilantes of yesterday's conventions and morality.

God's agenda for humankind has far more important things in store, and it calls forth from you and me a sincere determination to discern daily, what the Spirit of truth continues to reveal to us about the ways of Christ. It also calls forth from us, a modesty that acknowledges the need for each of us to hear other Christians share their discoveries, testing all of these beside the wisdom of the ages, beginning with the life of Jesus of Nazareth.

Listening rather than talking is what we need to do as the conventional forms of Christian community in the west are dissolving. Consider that the majority skin color of Christians has moved on from Mediterranean olive to Western European and North American white, has for the last few decades become overwhelmingly people of other colors: black, brown, and yellow. Church leaders and theologians from the *Global South* along with nations such as Korea, the Philippines and Malaysia, now set the agenda for world Christianity. Aided by rapidly developing technology, newer organizational forms and mission-oriented methods together hold promise in reinvigorating increasingly obsolete structures of Protestant denominations. If these structures survive they are going to become nearly unrecognizable to what we know now.

The promise of these changes ought to win our hearty embrace. Yes – the *Third World* has superseded the first and second. These beneficiaries of our missions and survivors of our colonialism, may just be that bread cast upon the waters returning to us fourfold. Let us trust what we pray is God's leading going forward, trusting that we are living into answers that glorify and further advance our Savior's fame.

Praying Twice

Exodus 15:20-21; Matthew 26:30; Ephesians 5:18-20

During the break at a continuing education event years ago, someone posed a question to all, *If you were to be whisked away to a desert island and along with your Bible you could take only one other book, which would you take?* Different theological classics were mentioned. And, I kid you not, someone actually said "The (Presbyterian) *Book of Order*. Though I knew nothing about him, I immediately felt sympathy for his wife. Then a freshly minted Presbyterian pastor, a rather spunky young woman said, *That is easy, I would take the hymnbook. Think of it,* she added, *the words alone make it the best devotional guide I know of. Wow,* I said, *I believe you're right!*

Today's introduction and dedication of our new hymnbook, *Glory to God* is also an occasion to celebrate First Presbyterian Church, New Bern's, strong and ongoing commitment to a significant and beautiful music program. The new music suite in the ministry center designed specifically for our seven choirs is as accommodating as any choral program could hope to have. The unsurpassed quality of our Fisk Organ together with the presence in the sanctuary of our carillon and its frequent use by our two hand bell choirs, give further evidence. Our desire has always been, and I pray always will be, that our music will glorify the God who caused David to play on his harp, the angels to sing at Jesus' birth, and Revelation's choir to gather around God's throne at the end of history.

For those in the congregation who do not like to sing except in the shower – and I fear your numbers are legion – I would have you consider how terribly lifeless our worship and faith would be without music. At a finance committee meeting at a previous congregation, a certain elder was overly eager not merely to prevent any increase, but to cut the music budget. At one point he said with some disdain, *I don't have an ear for music.* Another person simply asked him, *Well, would you want to live in a world without music?*[35] Whether you are expressing corporate praise or deep personal thankfulness, the enthusiasm that accompanies spiritual renewal or the need for comfort and consolation, strength and hope; singing praises to God expresses all of these. It was the greatest theologian of the first millennium, St. Augustine, who has been quoted as saying, *The person who sings prays twice.*[36]

Perhaps the oldest song extant, that is for which we have evidence, is still in print today. Following the Israelites miraculous escape from Pharaoh's chariots, Moses' sister Miriam, with tambourine in hand exclaims: *Sing to the Lord, for he has triumphed gloriously; horse and rider he has thrown into the sea.*" When Solomon led the Ark of the Covenant into the Temple, all the people were singing. In his second book, the Chronicler describes it by saying: *When the song was raised in praise to the Lord, the house of the Lord was filled with ...... the glory of the Lord.*[37]

---

[35] William R. Klein, *The Creed Revisited, Why Believe at All.* This from an unpublished series of sermons on the Apostles' Creed, preached at Second Presbyterian Church, Roanoke, Va., in the fall of 1985. p.18.

[36] http://wdtprs.com/blog/2006/02/st-augustine-he-who-sings-prays-twice/ In Augustine's work, the phrase *He who sings, prays twice* is not found. This sentence is as close as we have: *For he who sings praise, does not only praise, but also praises joyfully; he who sings praise, not only sings, but also loves Him whom he is singing about/to/for. There is a praise-filled public proclamation in the praise of someone who is confessing/acknowledging (God), in the song of the lover (there is) love."* Father John Zuhlsdort comments, *Augustine seems to say that when the praise is of God, then something happens to the song of the praiser/lover that makes it more than just any kind of song. The object of the song/lover in a way becomes the subject. Something happens so that the song itself becomes Love in its manifestation of love of the one who truly is Love itself.*

Instrumental music and hymnody came to fill the books of the Old Testament as a means of offering not only praise and Thanksgiving to God, but also to give voice to their urgent pleas in times of fear, despair and trouble. From David's harp, to the variety of instruments accompanying the singing of the Psalms in the Temple, we know our faith has always been a musical and singing faith.[38]

At the outset of the New Testament are the splendid songs of Mary, Zechariah and Simeon[39] expressing awe and wonder at our Savior's birth. We know that it was the practice of Jesus and the disciples to sing hymns together. In an off-handed comment at the conclusion of the Last Supper, Matthew wrote, *When they had sung a hymn, they went out to the Mount of Olives* (26:30).

Though we do not have the hymns of the primitive church, we find fragments cited in the letters of the Apostle Paul to the Church at Philippi, to Timothy and in John's first letter.[40] Even in Paul's hefty doctrinal statements are found verses of hymns that glorify God while expressing the assurances, the affirmations, the hopes and joys of our faith. We have evidence that the Lord's Prayer was early on set to music and sung in worship.[41] In the fifth chapter of the Letter to James the author links the singing of songs of praise with other activities such as praying, suffering, anointing and confessing. The Dean of Duke Divinity School, Gregory Jones says that in the Letter of

---

[38] 2 Chronicles 5:12-13

[39] Luke 1:46-55; Luke 1:68-79; Luke 2:29-32

[40] Philippians 2:6-11; 1 Timothy 2:5-6,16; 2 Timothy 2:11-13; 1 Jn 2:12-14

[41] SAVAE ANCIENT ECHOES CD by the San Antonio Vocal Arts Ensemble: *Music from the time of Jesus and Jerusalem's Second Temple* (World Library Publ: San Antonio, 2000) *Abwoon*, Lord's Prayer (Aramaic.

James, *to sing songs of praise (5:13c) is a sign of salvation that reflects God's abundant grace, rejoicing with his people in joy and sustaining those suffering bodily and spiritual pain.* In that same article entitled *Why are they singing?* Dr. Jones tells the story of a clergyman from Estonia eventually deported to Siberia during the Stalin era and executed. His journal was found later by friends and in it was his observation:

> *Today I am again reminded how little they understand us, and how little they understand our deepest longings for God's love. We have to disguise our Christian education with the children or the KGB will use our catechesis as an excuse to arrest us. Yet we couldn't disguise the children's singing hymns and songs of faith. We were afraid of their reaction, only to be surprised by their question. One of the officers came over to me and with a puzzled look asked: "Why are the children singing?"* He concludes, *They just don't get it, or are themselves afraid of it.*[42]

Sometime after the conversion of St. Augustine in the early fifth century, he wrote his old pastor about the days leading up to his conversion. He reminisced how he would sit outside the cathedral in Milan and listen. He wrote:

> *The tears flowed from me when I heard your hymns and canticles. The sweet singing of your Church moved me deeply. The music surged in my ears, and the truth seeped into my heart, and my feelings of devotion overflowed.*[43]

Among other things that recreate man wrote John Calvin, *music is the*

---

[42] *Why are they singing?* L. Gregory Jones, *Christian Century*, September 8-15, 1999, p. 864.

[43] Augustine, *Confessions*, transl. by R.S. Pine-Coffin, (Baltimore: Penguin Books, 1961), Book IX, Chapter 6, p. 190.

first...; and we should reckon it a gift from God intended for this use.[44] As the unity of the saints in heaven was held by Jonathan Edwards to be expressed through music, he saw its reality mirrored by the sacred music we sing here and now. He said,

> *The best, most beautiful, and most perfect way that we have of expressing a sweet concord of mind to each other is by music. When I would form in my mind an idea of a society in the highest degree happy, I think of them as expressing their love, their joy, their inward concord and harmony and spiritual beauty of their souls by sweetly singing with each other.*[45]

Edwards would have agreed with the contemporary poet, Mary Gordon, who wrote, *We sing to feel a world we can only imagine.*[46]

More recently, the Lutheran pastor and martyr Dietrich Bonhoeffer discusses hymn singing in a letter from his prison cell, to his friend Eberhard Bethge on March 27th of 1944. He writes:

> *It's a year now since I heard a hymn sung. But it's strange how the music that we hear inwardly can if we really concentrate on it (find that the) music acquires a 'new body'. There are only a few pieces that I know well enough to be able to hear them inwardly, but I get on particularly well with the Easter hymns.*[47]

---

[44] T.H.L. Parker, *John Calvin* (Batavia, IL: Lion Publ., 1975), p. 104.

[45] Thomas Schafer, ed., *The Miscellanies a-500*, #188, "HEAVEN." *Works of Jonathan Edwards*, Vol. 13, (New Haven: Yale, 1994), p. 331.

[46] Mary Gordon, *Circling My Mother: A Memoir*, (New York: Anchor; Reprint, 2008).

[47] Eberhard Bethge, ed. Dietrich Bonhoeffer, *Letters and Papers from Prison*, (New York: Macmillan Co., 1972), p. 240. See footnote #1 and notice that like Bonhoeffer who believes a hymn taken *inwardly* can acquire a *new body*, similarly,

It is said that the Sacraments pick up where words leave off; the very Word, enacted, or in the majestic words of the church: *visible signs of an invisible grace*. If that is true – and I believe it is – then singing and listening, is akin to a sacrament, for it succeeds at uniting our spirits with each other and with God's Spirit. Former Dean of Harvard Memorial Chapel, Peter Gomes, writes:

> *Where words fail, or at best divide, music succeeds at the.... ultimate level of communication... Among (those) singing, (I've known many to be) indifferent to theology, unmoved by the Bible, and in some cases hostile to religious faith, who are yet brought to the borders of heaven itself by the experience of singing the great choral music of the Christian West.* [48]

Indeed, throughout church history when the biblical message has been put to music to utter what our hearts hold and long for, the faithful have happily discovered that it has a persuasively edifying power of its own. Calvin was careful to say of church music, that *It should not be light and flighty like secular music, but with weight and majesty agreeable to the subject.* No parent I know likes the role of censoring what their children read, or watch or listen to, but given the society in which we live, we have no other choice. And when it comes to music I believe Calvin was on the mark when he cautions us by saying, *We must be careful of the words, for together with music, they have a secret and*

Augustine believes that "when the praise is of God, something happens to the song."

[48] Peter Gomes, *The Good Book: Reading the Bible with Mind and Heart*, (New York: Morrow & Co.,1996), p. 102. In Warren Goldstein, *William Sloane Coffin, Jr. A Holy Impatience*, (New Haven: Yale, 2004), In church *music should be a means of unlocking us, helping us to express joy and gratitude, poignancy, tenderness, courage, and love – all the great religious sentiment*, p. 136 (also, p. 88).

almost incredible power to move hearts one way or the other[49]

Four decades after the death of little known Etty Hillesum, came the publication of her diary. She began writing when imprisoned in Westerbork concentration Camp in the Netherlands, not far from the German border. It was the last stop before the gas ovens of Auschwitz would consume the estimated 100,000 Jews who passed through the doors of Westerbork. Poignantly, Etty began her diary at the same time as a little girl named Anne Frank who was hidden in a house only a few miles away. With degrees in Law and the Slavonic Languages, she was at the time war broke out studying psychology. Her diary *An Interrupted Life* is a testimony of faith and love written in the darkest hours of modern history. Upon its publication, it was quickly recognized as one of the great moral documents of our time.

In the face of impending death, Etty was the inspiration and consolation for many imprisoned with her. She bore marvelous witness to the inviolable power of love – being kind to her captors and refusing to condemn them – while reconciling her keen sensitivity to human suffering with an undimmed appreciation for the beauty and meaning of existence. It was, she believed, her vocation to redeem the suffering of humanity from within, by safeguarding what she called in one of her prayers, *that little piece of You, God, in ourselves.* In one of her last prayers she says to God:

> *I know that a new and kinder day will come. I would so much like to live on, if only to express all the love I carry within me. And I know there is only one way of preparing for the new age,*

---

[49] T.H.L. Parker, *Calvin*, p. 105.

by living it even now in our hearts.[50]

In early September of 1943 Etty was placed on the transport for Auschwitz where she would die two months later at the age of 29. When the transport first departed Westerbork in route to Auschwitz that September morning, from the window of the train she tossed out a card that simply read, *We left the camp singing…*[51]

So, let *us* practice now. For singing praise to God is not just an earthly testimony, it is even now an event brimming with eternity.

---

[50] Etty Hillesum, *An Interrupted Life and Letters from Westerbork*, (New York: Henry Holt & Co., 1996), p. 185.

[51] Hillesum, *An Interrupted Life*, p. 360.

Mutual Encouragement in the Faith

Psalm 133; Romans 1:8-15

In preparation for this day, I re-read several of Paul's letters and the second book of Luke, the Book of Acts. As Paul was regularly on the move from one congregation to the next, I was hopeful something of his experience would shed light on mine, as I leave one congregation to be with another, with you.

Paul possessed a terrific sense of God's presence and direction in his life. Whatever he did and wherever he went, was not based on a merely human decision. And so, we read in his introduction to the Christians at Rome that he was *asking that by God's will I may somehow at last succeed in coming to you.*

Let me tweak his lines a bit and say to you, the Saints of First Presbyterian Church that I rejoice that *by God's will, I have succeeded in coming to you.* I feel deeply and sincerely, that I have by God's will been called to minister with and among you. For like Paul, these things of God are not fortuitous, not left to chance. A cynic would conclude Paul' use of the phrase, *God's will*, was little more than a pious way of rubber-stamping his own decision. Everywhere Paul went he knew himself called, of being led. The same was true when the opposite occurred, when the divine calling took the form of divine prevention. He was called some places and prevented in going to others. *I have often intended to come to you* he tells the Romans, *(but thus far have been prevented)*...

When on his second missionary journey, Paul set his sights on Asia but, says *he was prevented by the Holy Spirit.* Next, we read of his effort to enter several Turkish provinces but was again thwarted *by the Spirit of Jesus.* That night, Luke says *a vision appeared to Paul: a man of Macedonia was standing beseeching him saying, Come over to Macedonia and help us.* And when he had seen the vision, Luke says *immediately we sought to go to Macedonia, concluding that God had called us to preach the gospel to them* (Acts 16:9).

Well my vision came in the form of e-mails and phone calls from members of the Pulpit Nominating Committee who spoke their own version, *Why don't you come over to New Bern and help us?* In time, in God's good time, the committee and you the congregation have as God's instruments, brought us to this moment.

In fact, my sense of being called to serve with you, preceded the phone calls and e-mails, even precedes this last go-round in your search for a pastor. My familiarity with your previous pastors and associates, my knowledge of your history and likely opportunities and challenges for the future, left an impression on me many years ago. I've had a sense, however irrational, that one day I would become your pastor. It was not that I aspired or desired the position, it simply struck me as inevitable.

What I want to say is something I hope will set the tone of ministry among you and with the rest of the staff, these words of Paul: *That we may be mutually encouraged by each other's faith, both yours and mine.* Authentic ministry always involves mutual encouragement: we are built up by one another's faith.

You may wonder how Paul could say that. Who could share with him anything about faith? *Brought up at the feet of Gamaliel*, the famous rabbi, and claiming himself as one *educated strictly according to our ancestral law, being zealous for God* (Acts 22:3). It was he who had the template experience of conversion when blinded by a vision of the Lord along the Damascus Road, followed by training the next three years in Arabia,[52] to return to become *God's chosen instrument to carry the Lord's name before Gentiles and kings and the people of Israel* (Acts 9:15). What, pray tell, did anyone have to share with him he didn't already know?

How about me? Do I see myself as your fearless leader, the professional Christian entirely knowledgeable in all the ways of the Christian Faith, called to be a minister of Christ's Church, educated beyond what common sense allows and my intelligence could take, and then coming out the expert? Hardly. Unlike our counterparts in medicine and law, clergy can never speak with authority about the mystery we call God. And theological education, important though it is, has limits, forever insuring that what it seeks to grasp will always exceed its reach. This is especially true as the subjective experience of faith, that is, one's life with God is impossible to suspend when considering the objective content of faith. The devotional and intellectual experiences of faith are both essential though most people pit them as polar opposites. And a theological education can exacerbate those differences between pulpit and pew, prompting William Sloane Coffin to warn graduates at Union Presbyterian Seminary's commencement exercises that *Education kills by degrees.*[53]

Nowhere is this more evident than in Scripture itself and the hard lesson Paul to learn. How upsetting it must have been for him to recall that it was the High Priest Caiaphas and the doctors of theology inciting the people and the Roman Procurator Pontius Pilate to put Jesus to death. Then he had to bear the guilt of his own complicity in the stoning to death

---

[52] Galatians 1:17.

[53] (Formerly Union Theological Seminary in Richmond, Va.), May 1978.

of Stephen.[54] It must have distressed Paul to consider that those who should have known the most knew the least. The objective content of their faith and the privilege and authority that went with it destroyed the genuine subjective experience of living in relationship with God. Only through living the faith can these separate dimensions merge into balanced Christian life. Here is a story that may shed some light on what I'm trying to say.

> *Early in the 19th century, in the days when the great fleets of sailing ships went out of New Bedford, Massachusetts, to scour the oceans of the world for whale oil, the most famous skipper of them all was a man named Eleazer Hull. Captain Hull took his vessel into more remote areas, brought home greater quantities of oil, and lost fewer crewmen in the process than any other master of his time.*
>
> *And all this was the more remarkable, because he had no formal navigational training of any kind. When asked how he guided his ship infallibly over the desert of waters, he would reply, Well, I go up on the deck, listen to the wind in the rigging, get the drift of the sea, and take long look at the stars. Then I set my course.*
>
> *One day, however, the march of time caught up with the ancient mariner. The insurance company whose agents covered vessels of Captain Hull's employers declared that they would no longer write a policy for any ship whose master did not meet certain formal navigational standards of education in the science of navigation.*
>
> *Captain Hull's superiors could understand this new rule. But*

---

[54] Acts 8:1

they were at a loss to know how to approach the proud man whose life had been spent on the bridge and tell him that he must either go to school or retire. After some consultation they decided to meet the problem head on. Three of the company's top executives went to Captain Hull and put their dilemma as tactfully as possible. To their amazement the old fellow responded enthusiastically. He had, it appeared, always wanted to know something about science, and he was entirely willing to spend several months studying it. So, the arrangements were made. Eleazer Hull went to school, studied hard, and graduated near the top of his class. Then he returned to his ship, set out to sea, and was gone for two years.

When the skipper's friends heard that he was putting into port again, they met him in an informal delegation on the docks. They inquired eagerly how it felt to navigate by the book, after so many years of doing it the other way.

It was wonderful Captain Hull responded. Whenever I wanted to know my position, go down to my cabin, get out all the charts, work through the proper equations with mathematical precision.

Then I'd go up on the deck, get the drift of the sea, listen to the wind in the rigging, and take a long look at the stars. Then I'd go back down to my cabin and correct my computations for error. [55]

The faith that gives life cannot be found in textbooks or the creeds of the churches, nor in some unusual conversion or mountain-top experience, not even in the mastery of biblical content. The faith that gives life is more caught than taught

---

[55] William Muehl, *All the Damned Angels* (Pilgrim Press, 1972, p. 16.

and it occurs through the mutual encouragement which is most evident in congregational life, namely the fruit of the spirit modeled by Christ: *love, joy, peace, patience, kindness, goodness, gentleness, faithfulness, humility and self-control* (Galatians 5:22-23).

It is this same spirit of Truth that will lead us into all the truth, who is the source of our mutual calling as a family of faith that draws us here together on each Lord's day to worship, and whose presence comes alive to us in word and sacrament. The necessary intellectual component to the Christian life can never be a substitute for the mystery at the heart of our faith: the presence and power at work in our lives and in the life of the world.

Several generations ago at New College, Edinburgh, Scotland, there was a great professor there named Robert Duncan. He was a saintly man and one of the great scholars of his age. So, learned was he that his students would joke and say that when he said his prayers at night, he spoke them in the classical Hebrew language. One night, as the story goes, two of his students slipped quietly outside the bedroom door of their professor to hear the great scholar at prayer. Expecting great words of wisdom spoken in Hebrew, this is what they heard:

> *Gentle Jesus, meek and mild,*
> *Look upon a little child.*
> *Pity my simplicity,*
> *Suffer me to come to Thee.*[56]

By the time Paul dictated his letter to Tertius to send off to Rome, he was no longer impressed by great knowledge, when after resorting to it in his debate with the Athenian

---

[56] This phrase is from a hymn by John Wesley.

philosophers on Mars Hill, he found himself spiritually powerless.[57] He knew enough to know how little he knew and there may be no greater knowledge than that. The knowledge he was unquestionably confident about was as simple as it was profound: *Jesus is the Christ of God, Lord and Savior of all.* Faith in Christ plays out in those places God leads us to enter, and through those persons God places in the path before us. Awaiting to be fulfilled through us on behalf of neighbors nearby and across the world, are the promises of God in the Gospel of Jesus Christ.

My earnest and unceasing prayer as long as providence allows, is that we will encourage, challenge, comfort and inspire one another, for the living of these days. Amen.

---

[57] Acts 17:22-18:1; 1 Cor. 2:1-5

Doing a "Beautiful Thing"

Matthew 26:6-13; Ephesians 1:15-23

To his angry disciples Jesus said of this unknown woman, *She has done a beautiful thing to me, (and) wherever the gospel is preached in the whole world, what she has done will be told in memory of her.* Why? What has she done to make her an example for us?

She takes a jar of perfume, a luxury imported from India, at a value equivalent to the annual wages of a laborer, and pours the whole flask, not a few drops, but all of it, on Jesus' head. Outraged, the disciples declare her wasteful. Had they discerned rightly, they would have noticed it was not ordinary waste; it was a *holy waste* for it grew out of the abundance of her heart. This woman is an example for us of the "ecstatic element" in our relationship with God.[58] She was overcome with wonder, thanksgiving, and praise.

The disciples represent the reasonable, sensible element in our relationship with God. As far as they are concerned, all waste has a common denominator. Indignant, they scold this woman saying, *(You) could have sold it for a large sum and given to the poor.* And yet, Jesus honors her action, and rebukes the disciples.

To be fair, the disciples' confusion is understandable. In line with the great tradition of Old Testament prophets, Jesus identified the divine heart with the powerless, the penniless, and those without voice in the halls of justice. And he lived as he taught that those who care for *the least of these* are caring *for me.* (Matthew 25:31f.) And now this! In one of the few stories

---

[58] Paul Tillich, *A Holy Waste* in *The New Being.* (New York: Charles Scribner's & Sons, 1955), p. 46.

found in all four gospels, Jesus' rebukes the disciples' appeal for the poor with what seems almost casual indifference, *you will always have the poor with you…*, he says. How can he say this? Why would he say it?

In Mark's Gospel, when the scribe asked him *Which is the greatest commandment?* Jesus replies *You shall love the Lord God with all your heart, soul, mind and strength, and You shall love your neighbor as yourself.* Jesus adds, *there is no other commandment* (notice, the singular), *than these* (notice, the plural). (Mark 12:29-31). By answering the scribes' question about the greatest commandment by giving not one, but two, then emphasizing their likeness by referring to both commandments in the singular, was Jesus way of underscoring their unity. So, we in the church have been taught that you show your love for God, through love of your neighbor. Therefore, the disciples, were taken aback at Jesus' lofty tribute to this wasteful woman, whose action took no apparent regard for needy neighbors. *Leave her alone,* Jesus says to those humanitarian disciples, *for she has done a beautiful thing to me.* Jesus' praise for her exceeds all others in the gospel.

This key is in the word *beautiful*. Primarily translated as something morally *good* or *right*, is here more appropriately translated in its secondary use as *beautiful*.[59] And what this woman did went even higher than ordinary notions of what is morally *good*, or in our common meaning of *beautiful*. For Jesus

---

[59] The preference for the earlier Revised Standard Version (RSV) has to do with the word κάλος in verse 10, translated as a *beautiful thing*. This is the aesthetic dimension Jesus is commending, adoration of the divine, that proves itself as the very source and wellspring out of which our love of neighbor is born and nourished. Lacking adoration of the divine, of beauty itself, eventually severs the source of the moral impulse to serve one's neighbor.

to hold her up as *the* example, wherever the Gospel is told in the world, ought to be enough to get our attention.

And this is the point: To give to the poor is right but the woman's deed belongs to a higher order of rightness. It was her complete uninhibited affection, overflowing into an uncalculating response of devotion, that is, worship. And worship in the eyes of the world, is, and always will be, a senseless waste.

The question comes up from the short-sighted who ask, *Why spend money on the Church when there are hungry people in the world?* The answer is not simply that worship is life's greatest experience but an unfailing fountainhead of generosity and selfless service. Devotion is a well, springing up eternally out of which flows great streams for the healing and blessing of humankind. The affection represented by that flask of perfume, the outgoing of affection and honor for Christ, has been the source of the greatest help to the poor the world has ever known. If we see life only in terms of money and grow deaf to – *You shall love the Lord your God* – soon there will not be the kind of persons willing to distribute any money at all.[60] If the 13 founders had chosen not to invest in this congregation by building this sanctuary but had given their money to the poor, the nearly 200 years of faith formation, Christian nurture, care, and, in particular benevolence in any form of service and financial generosity, would have never happened.

Though these two commandments are inextricably bound, one belongs to a prior order of rightness. When before the burning bush, Moses' sensed God's holy presence, his first act

---

[60] Halford E. Luccock, *The Gospel According to St. Mark, Interpreter's Dictionary of the Bible*, (Nashville: Abingdon, 1951), Vol. 7, p. 870.

was reverence; removing his shoes before the Living God.[61] It was out of that experience he received his call to lead the children of Israel out of Egypt. Our experience of worship is to evoke our awareness of the presence of the Holy, here in the place of your call that comes prior to service. This is where we return in the ongoing desire that the *eyes of our hearts be enlightened* (Ephesians 1:18), wherein we are commissioned anew for ministry. If you ignore the first, the second will follow. If you dam the river at it source, soon the bed will run dry. If you avoid the person and place where the marching orders are received, a generation or two later, all footsteps will cease.

While in graduate school a divinity student friend, a Presbyterian from Oklahoma, had a job with the city's welfare department, distributing food and clothing to those in need. I'll never forget one brief exchange between us. About his work he said, *You do know that this is what the church is really about.* I could only say to him, *If you actually believe that, you are in the wrong place. You don't need a Master's in Divinity, but a Master's degree in Social Work.*

In John's Gospel the story is identical to Matthew, Mark and Luke, except it is only Judas who objects to the woman's deed as being wasteful.[62] Like so many Judas, couldn't accept that Jesus was the *bread which had come down from heaven*. He only wanted someone to provide the daily bread of his miracles (John 6:35, 38, 41). *It was the devil, who tried to convince Jesus that we live by bread alone; anything else according to the evil one,*

---

[61] Exodus 3:2-6

[62] John 12:1-8

*is sinless excess.*⁶³

Jesus calls our waste on him and his body, the church, *holy*, our foolish extravagance, *beautiful*. The German poet Goethe was so very right when he wrote, *We should do our utmost to encourage the beautiful, for the useful encourages itself.*⁶⁴

While serving in Virginia Beach, I received a call from a Presbyterian Pastor in Norfolk, who needed us to join them in helping an immigrant family of seven, from Eastern Europe. Despite their education and the husband and father's highly employable skills, delays caused by the state department and the like, prevented them from finding work. Eligible for nothing, faced with a language barrier in a sea of strangers, their plight had truly become desperate. A deacon in our congregation took the family on what proved their first visit, she stopped at a florist and out of her pocket so as not to get in trouble with the church treasurer, purchased a dozen roses.

At a Presbytery meeting several weeks later, the pastor of First, Norfolk praised her to the high heavens. *Oh yes*, I said in my mundane little world, *the food and clothing for the children helped a great deal*. All the while he was shaking his head, *No, no* he said it was the *roses*.⁶⁵ That deacon addressed an even more basic need than hunger. By appealing to this woman's spirit to recognize and respond to beauty, our deacon helped restore her dignity. Hardly a waste; it was a *beautiful* thing.

These buildings – all of them, is our jar of *perfume*, our roses –

---

⁶³ William Willimon, *What's Right with the Church* (San Francisco: Harper & Row), p. 118.

⁶⁴ Christine Rosen. *Romance in the Information Age* in The *New Atlantis*, Winter, 2004.

⁶⁵ That deacon is the kindly saint, Anna Stewart.

used for study, fellowship and the many activities of which we are about, also represent our loving excess: especially this building. If the church is a business as some like to say, ours is a very inefficient use of the dollar, though none of us would dare spend a penny less. What we do here in particular is like that unknown woman, emptying the entire flask of costly perfume upon Jesus' head. To ask *What good does it do?* is like asking sweethearts *What good is hugging, kissing, singing and dancing?* It reveals how the questioner is already off track, for she or he cannot possibly understand what it means to be in love.[66]

In his first letter, John writes *We love, because we have been loved.* (1 John 4:19) So we know how to. The Apostle Paul says unless my love for others is born and nourished in my prior love for God, then it matters not if *I give away all that I have, and deliver my body to be burned, because I gain nothing.* (1 Corinthians 13:3)

What we do here is considered a low priority in the capitalistic equation of producing and consuming. And censorship of religion is one of the first acts of totalitarian regimes. Governments cannot allow such flights of human vision, permit its people to utter songs of what the heart holds, seek the beatific vision of God and His Kingdom as the only real world there is. What good would be such people to the godless state, with its flattened-out notions of human existence, where daily bread is the only bread. We just might end up troublemakers, *turn everything upside down* (Acts 17:6) and begin truly loving our neighbors. Our very presence here spread throughout the 400th block of New Street for all New Bern to see, represents a shadowy glimpse of the New Jerusalem. As the novelist John Updike once put it:

---

[66] William Willimon. *What's Right*, p. 117

> ...*my sense of things is that whenever a church spire is raised heavenward, though dismal slums surround it, hell, in all its forms is opposed by the rumor of good news, by an irrational confirmation of the wonder that is our birthright.*[67]

We no longer sing *Build thee, More Stately Mansions* because for years now, it is banks, courthouses, businesses and private residences, stadiums and coliseums that are examples of our excessive waste of love. It is only when it comes to the Church and all it visibly represents we are quick to cut corners, turn sanctuaries into multipurpose rooms, only here pleading economy behind a feigned concern for the poor. I fear for the legacy of faith we are leaving our children; telling them that we have new saviors and we build for them bigger and better homes.

My friends, this is what *The Third Century for First* Campaign is all about. Please join in, in whatever way you can, as we offer up this holy waste, this foolish extravagance. To continuing providing for this congregation to study, fellowship, pray, sing and worship, is to do a beautiful thing for our Lord.

---

[67] David H.C. Read. *The Faith is Still There* (Nashville: Abingdon, 1981), pp. 44-45.

How to Love God and Honor Your Country

1 Kings 22:1-40; Romans 13:1-7

Ahab, King of Israel is contemplating going to war with Aram, that is Syria. Israel will need an alliance with the southern kingdom of Judah if they are to be victorious. Our story picks up with Ahab's effort to persuade Judah's King Jehoshaphat to join him.

Jehoshaphat seems willing yet asks if Ahab has consulted his prophets. There are 400 and 1 of them. Ahab seeks the counsel of 400, who have all said, *Go up; for the LORD will give it into the hand of the king.*

The remaining prophet is Micaiah son of Imlah whom the King intentionally leaves out, explaining to Jehoshaphat, *I hate him for he never prophesies anything favorable about me.* But at Jehoshaphat's insistence, Ahab has Micaiah summoned. Surprisingly, the prophet does something he never does: Micaiah agrees with the 400 other prophets, making Ahab suspicious. The king says, in effect, *Quit 'pulling my leg' – tell me the truth.* Then, with graphic imagery he describes Ahab's defeat. The King doesn't like the prophecy, so he does what some congregations cannot do but might like to do when they don't like a sermon, he throws Micaiah into prison and likely to his death. Though vindicated by the outcome, power seldom admits to being wrong and shooting the messenger silences dissent.

Here is but one of several narratives in the Hebrew Scriptures about the tension that so often arises between preachers and politicians. Rooted in the unwavering conviction that God alone is Sovereign, religious leaders have had to remind political leaders of this, and the One to whom all are accountable now and ultimately. By honoring God first, at the cost of both his freedom and his life, who doubts that it was Micaiah who was the true patriot?

The counsel of the Apostle Paul to the Church at Rome seems to offer another side of a Christian loving God and honoring one's country when he says, *Let every person be subject to the governing authorities; for there is no authority except from God and those authorities that exist have been instituted by God.* The *law and order* types among us will claim that this is true patriotism.

Yet, I dare say that the Apostle writing in expectation of Christ's imminent return, believed his advice was going to be useful beyond a few days or weeks, perhaps only a couple of years. What is more, Paul is writing before the persecution of Nero at a time when authorities were tolerant of many religious beliefs among the people, provided they presented no threat to the Empire. No scholar I know suggests Paul's claim applies to Christians living under brutal tyrants, like Hitler, Stalin, Mussolini, Pol Pot Somoza, Khadhafi, Milosevic, Assad, and the like. Paul was not laying down a general rule applicable to every regime, ruler, president or king throughout history. If you think so, then you would have been a Tory during the American Revolution!

Besides, how else could Paul, a few verses earlier say to the Romans: *to present your bodies as a living sacrifice, holy and acceptable to God, which is your spiritual worship. Do not be conformed to this world, but be transformed by the renewing of your minds, so that you may discern what is the will of God – what is good, acceptable and perfect* (Romans 12:1-2).

The differences in loving God and honoring one's country would never be a problem if all governing authorities had been or are godly people, wisely discerning and acting to fulfill God's purposes. In fact, the very opposite has too often been true. There have been innumerable dictators and tyrants who have raped, tortured, and murdered the populace, enriching themselves at their people's expense. There have also been those otherwise morally upright and seemingly ethical leaders who nonetheless chose to ignore the needs of those victims of the underside of capitalism: the poor, the aged, women and children, those who have always been the most vulnerable in every society.

John Calvin, who believed obedience to one's leaders and governing authorities essential to being Christian, also said that when obedience to God is at stake, a Christian's duty is to resist and explore every avenue of reasonable and legally permitted protest.[68] Only then, can one be ready to discern whether the matter sufficient to commit what was and is called today civil disobedience.

As it pertains to the United States, George Stroup, professor of theology at Columbia Seminary, says that clergy in the historic Protestant denominations are more critical of government, more suspicious about and eager to call into question the policies and practices, believed inconsistent with the concerns of Christ. Thus, they are drawn to stories like Micaiah ben Imlah. On the other hand, it is the more conservative clergy and denominations who accept

---

[68] John H. Leith, The Reformed Tradition Atlanta: John Knox Press, 1977, pp. 204-5. Leith, writes, *In his perceptive biography of John Knox, Lord Eustace Percy has written that the best servants of the state are those whose highest loyalty was not to the state, but to God* (p. 72).

unquestioningly government decisions by pointing to Paul's words, that we are to be *subject to governing authorities*.[69] Stroup admits this is a gross generalization, yet my experience bears him out.[70]

So, who is with the 400 and who is with the 1? On any given issue it is most hard to say, as in the European Wars of the last four centuries, Christians were found on both sides, praying for victory in the confidence, God is surely on their side.

Who is the one, or who are the ones, who truly know how to love God and honor their country? To be a faithful Christian and a conscientious citizen, we need to keep these lofty allegiances in perspective. Yet, the authority we look to for that perspective already reveals which one we believe comes first. Christians begin with Jesus, particularly his summary of the commandments: *...you shall love the Lord your God with all your heart, and with all your soul, and with all your mind and with all your strength and mind. The second is this, You shall love your neighbor as yourself* (Mark 12:30-31a). Note, he doesn't say, "love your neighbor like God." He is saying, love your neighbor, but *not* as your god.

Jesus calls us to love God above all others – rulers, political regimes, political parties and governments. Professor Stroup adds, *too often those on the left and those on the right claim to be loving God with heart, soul, strength and mind, when in truth, it is the causes they so passionately embrace and love most.*

In 2006, our nation lost one of its most troubling prophets of

---

[70] George Stroup, *My Country 'Tis of Thee*, *Journal for Preachers* (Pentecost 2005), pp. 43f.

our generation, William Sloane Coffin. Awarded the honorary degree of Doctor of Divinity from his alma mater in 2002, President Levin also invited him back for the university to pull a prank on him, voting him the most controversial Yale graduate of the 20th century.

Coffin dropped out of college toward the end of World War II and served in Europe before, during, and beyond Germany's surrender. Later, in seminary, he was planning to drop out again and rejoin the army because as he told a friend, *I have this real old-fashioned belief that when your country goes to war, you serve your country.*[71] Before he re-enlisted, he was approached by the Central Intelligence Agency who needed him to fight North Korea through that agency.

After four years with the C.I.A., he finished divinity school, was ordained a Presbyterian Minister, and in a few years became the chaplain at Yale where he remained for 17 years. So popular was Coffin, that Gary Trudeau memorialized him through the 60's and 70's as the character *Rev. Sloane* in his comic strip, *Doonesbury*. Former Yale All-American and Dallas Cowboy great Calvin Hill said, *As a student none of my classmates wanted to be professional athletes or senators or scientists, we all wanted to be Bill Coffin.*[72]

Among the freedom riders to our segregated south in the early 60's, by the late 60's Coffin was leading the resistance to the draft in protest to the war in Vietnam, was arrested for conspiracy, though found not guilty. He would move on to become pastor of Riverside Church, New York. A fine preacher and accomplished concert pianist, Coffin was among

---

[71] Warren Goldstein, *A Holy Impatience*, p. 75.

[72] Warren Goldstein, *Yale Alumni Magazine*, March/April 2004.

the contingent of clergy sent by the U.S government to visit our hostages in the American Embassy in Tehran, Christmas1980. He retired as head of an organization he started called *SANE/FREEZE* (now *Peace Action*), that seeks a global ban on nuclear arms.

Shortly before his death, an interviewer began saying,

> *You have put your life on the line fighting against our nation's enemies in a foreign country, and you have served time in jail here in America when you believed our nation had become its own worst enemy. As a Christian minister can you tell us what you believe about loving God and honoring one's country?*

Through garbled speech as result of a stroke two years before, Coffin replied,

> *There are three kinds of patriotism, two that are bad, and one that is good. The first form is <u>loveless criticism</u>, those who do not appreciate what a great nation this truly is and can only find fault with it. It is to such persons I say, 'If you don't love America, go somewhere else, go to Canada, or wherever, just go. The second form is <u>uncritical love</u>, and to such persons who say, 'my country right or wrong,' I say the words of Jesus: 'For God so loved the world, he gave his only begotten son.' The third form is the best kind, the true patriots* he said, *are those who carryon a <u>lover's quarrel</u> with their country as a reflection of God's eternal lover's quarrel with the entire world.* (He emphasized) *Dissent is not disloyal, subservience is.*[73]

---

[73] William Sloane Coffin, *A Lover's Quarrel with America*, 26-minute DVD, www.olddogdocumentaries.com, New York, 2003, and Donald Shriver's introduction to Geicko Muller-Fahrenholz's book, *America's Battle for God: A European Christian Looks at Civil Religion* (Grand Rapids: Eerdmans, 2007).

In the writings of the early 5th century Bishop, Augustine, he says that one of the forms human sin takes is that of *concupiscence*. That four-syllable mouthful of a word means loving something too much or too little. We are, says Augustine, called to love appropriately. The Bible says the ability to love all worldly things appropriately, is derived from loving God first.

Having said that, let us offer our thanks for the United States of America. Let us remember with affection and the highest regard our fellow citizens down through the years and the sacrifices made this very day, by those whose love of country prompts them to serve in harm's way throughout our world.

This is a sweet, sweet land of liberty that we love and are proud to be her citizens, because there is much good about this country and any number of our values it upholds are worthy of emulation throughout the world. And as Christians, what stands higher than the freedom to worship, and the freedom to disagree on religious grounds? And as citizens, what stands higher than that we live in a nation where in the marketplace of ideas, democracy can work, and where alternative visions of who God would have us become as stewards of God's gifts are freely debated?

As Professor Stroup has noted: *We dare not love our country too much. That would be idolatry. But we dare not love it too little, for that would be ingratitude for God's gifts that come to us in many forms, including this country we call home.*[74]

---

[74] George Stroup, *Journal*, p. 45.

The Faith that Right Makes Might [75]

Matthew 7:12

With President's Day tomorrow coinciding with the 200th anniversary of Abraham Lincoln' birth, I have chosen to preach on his life and faith. In fact, I'm preaching about God but leaning heavily on Lincoln's life as illustrative of one who recognized God's providence in the events of his day. Don't let it disturb you that I'm a Virginian by birth and whose middle name is *Lee*. I do so – gladly – as Lincoln's knowledge and keen insight into the meaning of Scripture surely matched or exceeded the clergy of his day. Lincoln was hardly an orthodox Christian. As far as we know was never baptized, though he did grow up in attending a Baptist Church. He was not a Presbyterian though he attended Presbyterian services most of his adult life. He wasn't a Catholic though attempts have been made to claim him for Rome. And if we believe Mary Todd Lincoln who ought to have known, he never professed to be a Christian.[76]

Why then a sermon on Lincoln? Well, if George Washington is the Father of our Country, it is no less true that Abraham Lincoln is the Spiritual *Father Abraham*, of the American soul. No President embodied greater devotion to "nature's god" and in a way more Christ-like than any of our Presidents before or since, and certainly more so than most of the clergy of his day north or south of the Mason-Dixon line. Lincoln grasped the biblical drama of sin and redemption with startling clarity. And

---

[75] Jon Meacham in *American Gospel: God, the Founding Fathers, and the Making of a Nation*. (New York: Random House, 2006, p. 119.

[76] Gerald J. Prokopowicz. *Did Lincoln Own Slaves: And Other Frequently Asked Questions About Abraham Lincoln*. (Vintage Civil War Edition, 2009), p. 31.

ironically, his assassination on Good Friday gives a near transcendent feeling of a blood atonement the war seemed to require of him.[77] As if the death of one of his sons in battle, wasn't already enough.

When facing the greatest conqueror Europe had ever known, Winston Churchill told his countrymen *I have nothing to offer but blood, toil, tears, and sweat.* Churchill said nothing Abraham Lincoln hadn't already known, lived and given, in his singular achievement of preserving the Union. At the same time Lincoln proved Churchill right: *History judges a man*, he said, *not by his victories or his defeats, but by their results.*[78] And by the means to an end, that end being the union preserved, Lincoln spoke to the nation in his first inaugural saying, *Let us have faith that right makes might, and in that faith, let us, to the end, dare to do our duty as we understand it.*

While he lacked formal education, the political acumen of this gangly rail-splitter from Illinois by way of Kentucky, had few if any equals in his day, and perhaps of any day. Why was that? It was in part because as he told a crowd at Independence Hall one month after becoming President, *I have never had a feeling politically that did not spring from the Declaration of Independence.*[79] This is why four years later he thought nothing of ignoring a delegation of Ohio and Illinois clergymen petitioning him to seek a new preamble to the U.S. Constitution. This preamble would declare, and I quote: *the Lord Jesus Christ.... Ruler among the nations.... (whose) revealed will (is)... of supreme authority, is in order*

---

[77] Mark Noll. *America's God: From Jonathan Edwards to Abraham Lincoln.* New York: Oxford, 2002, p. 429..

[78] William Manchester, *The Last Lion: Visions of Glory* 1874-1932, (New York: Little & Brown, 1983), p. 6, p. 44.

[79] Jon Meacham, *American Gospel,* p. 114-115.

to constitute a Christian government, to form a more perfect union.[80] As George Washington and those who shaped our government knew, only *nature's god* or *the god of liberty*, which is a god only generally known, could be sufficiently comprehensive to include *every* American.

If failure to affirm Christ in words made him seem less than Christian, Lincoln's cooperation with the Spirit of Christ in seeking liberty and justice for all, made him Christian. Jesus once said, *Not everyone who says to me 'Lord' 'Lord,' will enter the kingdom of heaven, but only the one who does the will of my Father in heaven.* (Matthew 7:21) Similarly, in the parable of the two sons; the first one who said no to his Father's will then changed his mind and did it, was the one who proved faithful.[81] It is in this sense Lincoln was Christian, or doing the will of God. Scripture repeatedly gives evidence of God using outsiders as his chosen instruments, though evidence of this often escapes the impoverished logic of many insiders.[82]

Lincoln's greatness ought not allow us to overlook his wit. He found it humorous for example, that General George McClelland's correspondence always began with the words: *From Headquarters – In the Saddle.* Lincoln said, *'It is strange how the General puts his headquarters where everyone else puts their hindquarters.'*[83] But it was his compassion for his countrymen that set him apart for true greatness. To a mother who lost several sons in the same battle, Lincoln sent a note as moving

---

[80] Jon Meacham, *American Gospel*, p. 130.

[81] Matthew 21:28-31.

[82] Reinhold Niebuhr, *The Nature and Destiny of Man*, Vol II, *Human Destiny*. (New York: Scribners, 1964), p. 122.

[83] William Wolff, *The Almost Chosen People: A Study of the Religion of Abraham Lincoln*, (New York: Doubleday, 1958, pp. 97.

as you will ever read or hear. He said:

> *I feel how weak and fruitless must be any words of mine which should attempt to beguile you with the grief of a loss so overwhelming. But I cannot refrain from tendering to you the consolation that may be found in the thanks of the Republic they died to save.*
>
> *I pray that our Heavenly Father may assuage the anguish of our bereavement, and leave you only the cherished memory of the loved and lost, and the solemn pride that must be yours, to have laid so costly a sacrifice upon the altar of Freedom.*[84]

No President has waxed more lyrical. Fired by the conviction which could only belong to one who had faced down his own inner demons, he possessed an inflexible resolution and readily imposed his will and imagination on the Union. [85] As his Gettysburg Address is ample evidence, Lincoln like Churchill, *was an intuitive genius who knew how to gather the blazing light of history into his prism, and then distort it to his own ends. …. 'Political genius,' said Otto Von Bismark, 'consists of hearing the distant hoof beat of the horse of history and then leaping to catch the passing horseman by the coattails.'*[86] This was who Lincoln was, and this was what he did.

And he did so against odds that would break ordinary souls. No President has ever inspired more hatred among Americans than Abraham Lincoln. In 1860, he didn't get a single vote in 10 southern states, and only 40% of the popular vote. His election induced seven states to secede before his inauguration.

---

[84] Jon Meacham, *American Gospel*, p. 122.

[85] Joshua Wolff Shenk, *Lincoln's Melancholy: How Depression Challenged a President and Fueled His Greatness* (Mariner: Boston), 2006.

[86] William Manchester, *The Last Lion*, pp. 19, 44.

If this wasn't bad enough, during the war he was vilified in the North for his weakness and incompetence. And yet 200 years after his birth, no president is dearer to a genuine American Patriot than Abraham Lincoln, his enduring appeal noted in the over 15,000 books written about him to date.[87]

Yes, he had clay feet like the rest of us, and aspects of his political sagacity were at times questionable, but it must be with some pause we in the 21st century judge someone from the 19th century.[88] Besides, compared with today's politicians Lincoln's personal life as husband and father was pristine. And so, I commend to you this day, the Christ-like spirit with which Lincoln lived out his belief that *right* makes *might*, by way of his 1) *charity*, by the 2) *absence of self-righteousness*, and by his Presbyterian 3) *view of Providence* he learned I suppose, from attending services.

As it pertains to his charity, consider his second inaugural. Barely two months before his assassination, Lincoln said:

> *With malice toward none; with <u>charity</u> for all; let us strive to finish the work we are in; to bind up the nation's wounds; to care for him who shall have borne the battle, and for his widow and orphan.*[89]

Lincoln's appeal you notice was not restricted on behalf of the Union soldiers, widows, and orphans or those who had only suffered for the Union. He meant it for all: Confederate and

---

[87] *The Chicago Tribune* editorial, February 12, 2009.

[88] Historian Ron Blight says it well, *Remembering is always to some degree about forgetting*. PBS Interview by Louis Gates on Lincoln's 200th birthday aired on WUNC, 12 February 2009.

[89] Mark Noll, *America's God*, p. 427.

Union alike. In fact, Lincoln was careful to never give into the common parlance of referring to the southern states as *Confederate* or speak of secessionists as if they were anyone other than fellow countrymen. He claimed that the *peculiar institution* as slavery was called, had originally come to the south by way of British and Yankee slave traders, and it was the sin of a nation and only an accident of circumstance that the southern economy had come to be dependent on slaves.[90] But Lincoln's charitable attitude was held by only the slimmest minority in the north bent on vengeance. It is no small irony that southern sympathizer John Wilkes Booth succeeded in robbing the south of their most important friend, with whom the era of Reconstruction would have been quite different.

Lincoln's magnanimous and charitable attitude struck a chord that ought to be etched in every American: that the winners of war need to get over their victory, just as surely as the losers need to get over their defeat. How much bloodshed history would have been spared recording, had such charity been available from gracious victors! How many in a position to forgive has withheld this gift to create heart-rending divisions between friends and communities!

Lincoln also refused any notion of the Union possessing a monopoly on *virtue*. When a young adjutant jubilantly greeted Lincoln with news of a victory claiming that surely God must be on our side, Lincoln corrected the officer saying, *Sir, my concern is not where or not God is on my side; my greatest concern is to be on God's side, for God is always right*. Lincoln countered every attempt to demand of the nearly defeated foe, admission of full guilt, as if only southerners had to repent. And though he

---

[90] William Wolff, *The Almost Chosen People*, p. 103. Southern Presbyterian theologian, Robert Dabney was to echo Lincoln's point nine months afterward.

claimed to be acting on the good he knew, he always qualified his assessment before the higher standard of God's judgments that were alone *true and righteous altogether*. He said:

> *Both read the same Bible and pray to the same God, and each invokes his aid against the other. It may seem strange that any men should dare to ask a just God's assistance in wringing bread from the sweat of other men's faces; but let us judge not that we not be judged. The prayers of both could not be answered – that of neither has been answered fully.* [91]

Only someone who sees reality clearly can speak and act with the humility of Lincoln. In this spirit, Lincoln appealed to the national conscience to be receptive to as he called it, *the better angels of our nature*[92] and in that we shall find the promise of our own destiny, and not with a self-righteousness that only engenders future hostility.

What separated Lincoln even more from the professional theologians of his day however, was his view of *Providence*. Following the Union's second defeat at Manassas, Va., in 1862, Lincoln wrote in his diary what he titled: *A Meditation on the Divine Will*. Intended for no other eyes than his, it is a most remarkable theological commentary on the war. He writes:

> *The will of God prevails. In great contests each party claims to act in accordance with the will of God. Both may be, and one must be wrong. God cannot be for, and against the same thing at the same time. In the present civil war, it is quite possible that God's purpose is something different from the purpose of*

---

[91] Mark Noll, *America's God*, p. 427. (Matthew 7:1)

[92] Madeline Albright. *The Mighty and the Almighty: Reflections on America, God, and World Affairs*. HarperCollins, 2006, chapter 19, pp. 293f.

> *either party – and yet the human instrumentalities, working just as they do, are of the best adaption to affect His purpose. I am almost ready to say this is probably true – that God wills this contest, and wills that it shall not end yet. By his mere quiet power, on the minds of the now contestants, He could have either saved or destroyed the Union without a human contest. Yet the contest began. And having begun He could give the final victory to either side any day. Yet the contest proceeds.*[93]

Over the course of the war, Lincoln's view of providence was further developed along the lines of a much more *primordial vision*,[94] that is to say, in keeping with the Bible. Free from the taint of an Americanism first trumpeted by John Winthrop's *City set on a Hill*, Lincoln boldly challenged *American exceptionalism*. While preachers of the day saw the war to save the nation as further proof of our being chosen as God's new Israel, Lincoln's larger perspective saw the same cycle of unredeemed human nature at work having its way.

A Lincoln parable of our fallen nature was shared by an Illinois legislator after his death. Once when his sons were small, the congressman happened upon Lincoln walking with his two sons one on each side, pleading desperately with their father. When asked about the source of their distress, Lincoln replied: *The problem with my sons is the problem of the whole world. I have three walnuts in my pocket and each boy wants two.*

Preachers of the day also believed the meaning of providence to be easily transparent and knowing the knowledge of God's will added confidence that they could take control and determine the course of events. (Sound familiar?) In Lincoln's

---

[93] Mark Noll, *America's God*, p. 431.

[94] Mark Noll, *America's God*, p. 430.

honesty and humility, he rightly claimed God's providence opaque, and impossible to discern at any point in time, and to believe otherwise was to inflate one's pride at claiming to know what only God could know. The legacy of Lincoln provides for you and me, the best lesson of the relationship of a theologically informed life as a citizen. His life was lived in a way that gave hope that our nation might one day truly be, as Lincoln declared her, *God's Almost Chosen People*.[95] The promise of his witness, unorthodox as it may have been, points us back to the Bible, the source of wisdom from which he deeply imbibed.

---

[95] William Wolff, *The Almost Chosen People*, p. 3.

Marriage Service
Robert Bressler & Leah Hawkins

Moments ago, coming down the aisle arm-in-arm with my daughter Leah each wearing the gown of our choice, it occurred to me to begin by stating the obvious: I'm wearing two hats today. My life as father now gives way to my role as minister, but as you can see, I'm not a quick-change artist! Having performed nearly 200 weddings it is the first for me to begin in the Narthex unsuccessfully trying to get my heart off my sleeve and back into my chest. It is also a first for me to anticipate needing help. So, for safety's sake I brought the cavalry with me in the form of Bill Klein, friends since our youth, and his wife Deb, friends since our later youth. Ever since their toddler days our Abigail and Leah have called them "Uncle Bill" and "Aunt Deb."

Rob and Leah, at last we are all here! You are both here to commit yourselves one to another before God, your families and the rest of this glad company. I remind you also present with us are all those you and your families have loved and lost, yet only for a time. If you listen closely you'll hear their silent voices joined with ours in giving their blessing; Rob –Grandma Betty and Pops on your father's side and Papa on your mother's side; Leah – Grandmas and Grandy, on my side, and your mother's brother Uncle Mark whom you never got to know.

So, it is then with one voice – as the old hymn puts it – that *brother, sister, parent, child, friends on earth and friends above*[96] – are all

---

[96] *Glory to God: The Presbyterian Hymnal* (Louisville: Westminster/John Knox Press, 2013), *For the Beauty of the Earth*, #14, 4th stanza.

committing to uphold you in the promises you are making to God and each other.

You say that it is love that brings you here and you are right. God has placed his providential calling at the very center of your mutual attraction. And now it is that you've come to formalize what you have both realized: your mutual need to complete and find your completion in each other. It is God, then, who unites the two of you to the exclusion of all others as the church walls tell us, *till death do you part*. So, while it is God's love that creates your marriage it is your marriage that will teach you what a costly adventure love is, as it unfolds in ever new and unpredictable ways. It will prompt each of you to consider your individual past, in anticipation of your future together.

The questions I will soon be asking you are not to discover how at this moment you feel about each other. I think everyone here has a pretty good idea about that. However, it is with an eye toward your future together that the answers you give will come in the form of a promise. These promises you will be asked to make are to each other about the kind of person you desire to become for God and your life's partner. Before that, I have a few things to say.

Given the demanding nature of your respective professions you need to hear this, perhaps first. In every congregation I have served I've had members actively employed and retired from literally all walks of life, farmers, watermen, electricians, plumbers, bricklayers, men and women from every business, and from every profession, lawyers, judges, surgeons to hospital administrators, theologians and biblical scholars. I've had military – from buck private to rear admiral; I've had them from the government – from the groundskeeper at the governor's mansion to a United States Senator, and I've had them from most academic positions you can think of from preschool to college president. I've had as members Pulitzer Prize Nominees, All-American Athletes, Beauty Queens, an Olympic gold medal winner, and yes, even a trapeze artist. Among them are those married once, twice, three times, and those who gave up and simply lived together; those who are single, divorced, widowed and widowers, sometimes once, twice and three times over. When visiting with them I ask about their families of origin and their own families, those with and without children, grandchildren and great-grandchildren. I also talk with them about what it was they did for a living, what it required of them, and what satisfactions if any their work provided. In all my years, with all those I have been privileged to talk with, I never heard one say, *I regret not putting in more time at work.... If only I had pushed ahead, and if necessary spent less time with my wife and children, it would have been worth it. I wouldn't have been overlooked every time there was a promotion had I done so.*

Never heard anything like it. No, the regrets I have heard and still hear but the very opposite. May neither of you make that mistake unless you want these tragic and painful words written over the tombstone of your family relationships ... *Too late.*

It was years ago Leah, when your mother and I received our premarital counseling from Uncle Bill's father. Because he said something that day I have found to be consistently true over 34 years as husband and pastor, I want to pass it on to you and Rob. It was 1976 so my recollection of are in my words, and I share them in the hope of communicating something of the spirit we experienced as well.

Ask anyone who has ever walked down the aisle and promised *to love and honor......as long we both shall live*, and they'll tell you that you'll soon discover it takes an inordinate amount of grace, patience, forgiveness, maturity, not to forget a sense of humor, to live up to that promise.

Whenever I talk to couples planning to marry, I tell them that the only real resources they have for a successful marriage are the lives they bring to it. *If* as you grew up you cultivated only selfishness, self-indulgence and the moral blindness that blames others for whatever goes wrong; *if* you have never learned what it means to give of yourself, to be faithful and trustworthy, to honestly see yourself as the Bible says you are, and to be forgiving, *then* you are not prepared for marriage. And neither expert counseling, nor encouragement and guidance from parents, friends and mentors can give you those lost resources. Of course, the church has a limitless source of grace, patience, forgiveness and maturity, but it's not a magical potion someone can give you. These graces must be drawn upon and built into who you are over your lifetime or they're useless. I have found this is true not only in your married and family life, it is equally so in your personal and professional lives. Either you prepare for the great events of your life that typically arise suddenly and unexpectedly, or you will not be equal to the challenges that will surely come.

Ask anyone who has been married for a long time. They will likely tell you that they are no longer married to the person they once thought they were marrying. Five years from now or ten years from now, the person standing next to you won't necessarily be the person you thought you were giving yourself to. This is in part why the world-renowned ethicist Stanley Hauerwas from Duke says that *you always marry the wrong person.*[97]

---

[97] John Berkman and Michael Cartwright, ed., *The Hauerwas Reader* (Durham: Duke University Press, 2001), p. 513.

Not exactly but hear me out. Think about it: marriage is a peculiar predicament because if it requires you to choose just exactly the right person…… you're in big trouble for the *right person* very soon becomes a moving target. Marrying means promising to be faithful to someone who is continually changing even as you will be! Therefore, the church will not ask Rob <u>*do you*</u> *love Leah*, but rather "Rob <u>*will you*</u> *love Leah? – Leah* <u>*will you*</u> *love Rob?* Your marriage ought to keep you on your toes for you will forever be learning to grow in that love to the person you marry today.

The Ethicist Gilbert Meilander has written that finally,

> …… *it is holiness that God is after. And so, in marriage God goes to work on you, begins to teach you what it means, what it will require of you, to love just this one person as God loves each of us with unwavering, indeed steadfast faithfulness. And yet, this can only happen as we accept the discipline of marriage as God's good gift to us, that is, to you.*[98]

So, may it be: that God blesses you with conspicuous joy and length of days together – so when others look at your marriage they will see what joy looks like. And may all be aware that the utter beauty of it is all God's doing, and why it is so marvelous in the eyes of us all.

---

[98] Meilander's words come from an article in the *Christian Century*.

Marriage Service

Max Frumes & Abigail Hawkins

Out of two faith traditions Judaism and Christianity, Max and Abigail have come. They have pledged their willingness to learn together the faith of what each has to say, valuing their differences, confirming throughout that their being together is far more pleasing to God than should they remain apart.

Abigail and Max, be aware in these moments of those absent from our number, but we pray are present in spirit; family members from generations gone by and those from your own. Though their voices are silent now if you listen closely you can hear theirs join ours in calling upon God's blessing for you to keep the promises you are making this day. Max —your father's parents, Norman and Ida Frumes, your mother's parents, Claire and Robert Blackington cousins Libby Oppenheim, Florence Weinlos Soifer and Anna Louis, Uncle Robert Blackington and your great Uncle, Manny Louis. Abigail – My parents, George and Jane Hawkins, and on your mother's side, her father, Gene Krumnacher and your mother's brother, your Uncle Mark, and your grandmother, Nana, who wanted so much to be here today.

The Book of Genesis tells us something about this. The first of the two creation stories where we are told that *God created the human* (then it reads), *in God's own image God created them; male and female God created them* (Genesis 1:26-27; 5:1-2). Note the need for both genders to realize God's image, not one without the other. God's image is realized in relationships between the genders. This is what the rabbis of old and the primitive church fathers and mothers, together knew, believed and taught. They still do. God's image exists wherever male and female live in mutual regard for each other.

The supreme example of this regard has historically believed to be found in the marriage of husband and wife. Yet this creation story is about the building blocks for how human society began and flourished. The realization of God's image has to do with the respect and harmony between the genders in every relationship of male and female: Father–daughter; Mother–Son, the mix of genders in extended family relationships, co-workers, neighbors, friends, and strangers, are to honor the image of God that understands the other gender is needed for any to make transparent God's image. It is both genders. Consider the centrality of this egalitarian regard claimed for at the beginning of human society. How have we let it go astray? Given the subservient role women have had to suffer at the hands of Jewish and Christian males, realize how the teaching of ancient Scripture still remains ahead of at least three-quarters of today's world.

In the other, earlier account of creation is found in the second chapter of Genesis. It is said that God desires for "the *Adam* or *the human* to have a *helper* or more precisely the Hebrew means one *fit* for the human. To be a helper, to be *fit* for each other is specified in these three ways: 1) to be *equal to*, not one above or one below the other; 2) to be *adequate for*, to hear and be heard, a willingness to share, to enter in both the joys and travails of the other as if it is happening to you; and 3) to be *different from* means that while you become *one flesh* you are still uniquely you and your differences are to complement and strengthen both of you as together you enjoy and endure the unexpected and unanticipated changes of life as God's awaiting providence unfolds.

In the Old Testament, marriage was primarily for the propagation of the race and to protect inheritance rights and lands owned by the extended families of the tribe. You can forget worrying about matters of passing on real estate, at least as long you live in New York City. As to propagating the race you'll need no scriptural warrant. When it comes to producing babies both parents will, if necessary, provide you all the encouragement you'll ever need.

In the New Testament, the purpose for marriage changes significantly. Marriage becomes a *vocation,* that is, *a calling*. I know this is going to sound quaint to modern ears, but I'm going to say it anyway. For Jesus, the Apostle Paul and in the teaching of the church through the centuries, a Christian marries only because each finds it personally necessary to continue growing in faithfulness and discipleship. God's gift of marriage is not intended to make us happy, but to make us holy. Of course, in the long run, genuine happiness only comes through holiness.

It is God's providential leading bringing the two of you together that we are here to offer our thanks and to celebrate. We are grateful for what each of you has found in the other as we celebrate with you the promise of what your marriage and life can be, from this day forward.

Max, even now, you have talents and gifts of which you are unaware, that will lie dormant, unless Abigail is by your side, who by simply being the woman you love, will release unknown gifts and undiscovered talents in you.

The same is true for you, Abigail. With Max by your side, by simply being the man you love, will release in you unknown and undiscovered talents and gifts. And it gets even better, for in the life God has destined for you both, God becomes glorified through your marriage which occurs at the very intersection of your highest happiness.

Max, a very fine woman has chosen to cleave unto you as to no other. Do not let the sun set from this day forward without thanking God for her.

Abigail, a fine young man has chosen to cleave unto you as to no other. Do not let the sun set from this day forward without thanking God for him.

And never forget, this is God's doing, and why it is so marvelous in the eyes of us all.

Memorial Service

Mark Raymond Krumnacher

In his book, *A River Runs Through It,* Norman MacLean writes about his Presbyterian minister father, his mother and younger brother, about religion and fly-fishing in Missoula, Montana. The family story as MacLean tells it, swirls around the exploits of the younger brother whose entire life was one that led inexorably to his destruction and death. Try as they might, the family members were little more than helpless bystanders.

In one of his father's last sermons several years after his younger son's death and not long before his own, are heard echoes of pain and a reaching out for consolation. To his congregation he preached saying...

> *Each one of us here today will at one time in our lives look upon a loved one in need and ask the same question, "We are willing to help Lord, but what if anything is needed?" Where it is true, we can seldom help those closest to us; either we don't know what part of ourselves to give or often, the part we have to give is not wanted. And so, it is those we live with and should know who elude us, but we can still love them. We can love completely without complete understanding.*[99]

Who among us here today has not experienced the same with Mark, whose untimely death shocks us, but does not surprise us. None of us knew what part of ourselves to give, or, as we all came to feel, the part we had to give was not wanted. If our

---

[99] Norman MacLean, *A River Runs Through It.* (Chicago: University of Chicago Press, 1976), pp. 112-113. *A River Runs Through It,* Columbia Pictures, Inc. 1992, a film by Robert Redford.

sense of inadequacy to help him in this life was frustrating, our wondering what to think and how to feel in his death is no less so.

I knew him as a little boy, even then more to himself than most would think natural, yet unable to conceal his easy good looks, nor his athletic talent and academic prowess to whom both also came effortlessly. Even more tragic then that the knots down deep, deeper than he or anyone else could go, deprived an occupation of his intelligence and skill, and a family, perhaps a family of his own, of his love and affection. With what he had in himself to become and in what became of him, let there be no pretense of good news. And why is this? Can this turn on any one thing that anyone can point to? Perhaps. Bill Ellenbogen's explanation may be the most accurate. As he told me only yesterday *We certainly liked Mark around here if we could only have gotten him to like himself.*

But someone more important not only liked but loved him, who always loved him completely, and with complete understanding. Concerning their brother Lazarus, both Mary and Martha in separate conversations with Jesus said, *Lord if you were here my brother would not have died* (John 11:21,32c). We could I suppose say the same. Yet, I cannot and will not believe that though beyond our reach, he was ever beyond the grasp of our heavenly Father. More the tragedy for him, that God's love was unknown to him. I take my consolation and would suggest you do the same in knowing that when Mark's heart stopped beating, God's heart was the first heart to break.

Now, there are many who confess the Christian Faith that would deny what I have just said. They are the ones who believe only in a god whose sovereignty can be reduced to the confines of their limited imagination, and a god whose mercy is restricted to their own moralistic rule-making and setting of boundaries, beyond which the love and mercy of our Lord does not reach. The litmus test for those eligible, for the insiders, is usually found in one text popular at funerals, it is in John 14, where Jesus says, *No one comes to the Father, except through me* (6b). Some verbal acknowledgment of Christ's Lordship, whether sincere or not, is for many the needed guarantee of salvation, as if the words themselves function like some magical incantation. Mark likely never professed to this, at least not in the hearing of any of us.

Now Jesus' claim, *No one comes to the Father, except through me*, is as true as true can be, provided you don't limit the possibilities of how and when Jesus communicates this truth in the lives of others. God's ways of accomplishing God's will in our lives, and the way Christ ushers us into the divine presence is unique to each. Beyond our own experience and those like us, we ought not to pretend *our way* with Christ, is Christ's only way with everyone. Our God is one whose ways are past finding out. On this matter, agnosticism is the surest sign of faith. When it comes to others, it is best we not pretend to know what only God can know.

Several years ago, I stood by the grave of a troubled man who drank himself to death. He was never a member of a church, never got it together in his life, never figured it out. Together with family and the few friends, I stood at the grave in awkward sadness, circumstances not unlike ours at this very moment. What would you have said? Would it be Jesus' words, *No one comes to the Father except through me?* Or are there other words equally true and more appropriate.

You heard me earlier reading: *that God our Savior, desires everyone to be saved and come to the knowledge of truth*, (1 Timothy 2:4; 2 Peter

3:9) and Jesus himself saying, *It is not the will of my Father that one of these little ones should perish* (Matt. 18:14). And, as old John says in his first letter, *Jesus is the one sent by the Father to be the Savior of the world* (1 John 4:14). Though John, in his gospel can sound so exclusive, even here Jesus is heard to say, *I have other sheep who are not of my fold and I am going to bring them in also* (10:16).

Whatever else that can be said, surely the proper position of the Christian is to count on the mercy of God, and to trust that God's everlasting arms are now embracing this one who eluded us. We are to live in the confidence that the peace he never found in this life has given way to *the peace that passes all understanding* (Philippians 4:7). If heaven is not permitted him, I dare say it is a place fit for any of us. If his family and friends could not reach him, none here, the Church in particular, dare judge him.

But who then is guilty and who is innocent? No one, and everyone. Bound up together as we are in this bundle of life we remain nonetheless a collection of isolated individuals, who alone must make choices, live the consequences; be accountable. The Apostle Paul speaks to this matter in Galatians 6 in what on the surface appears a contradiction. In verse 2 he says we are *to bear one another's burdens*, but in verse 5 says, *everyone must carry their own load*. The apostle assumes we know each to be true and to trust God's Spirit to discern which to be the truth at the right time. Somewhere in our efforts to enter Mark's burden and help him *bear* it and to stand aside and allow him to *carry his own load,* either the right time never came or more likely, we missed it. Along with Mark, we dropped what was ours to bear, and stumbling, he chose a path that has led us here today.

We need forgiveness and so does Mark. Believe in the good

news of the Gospel, in Jesus Christ, we are all, *all of us*, forgiven.

In Ernest Hemingway's novel, *A Farewell to Arms*, Frederic Henry is an ambulance driver in the First World War. The trials he endured, the wounds he suffered, the waste and the killing of what is good, kind and noble, have left him desolate. He ruminates and says somewhat hopefully, *The world breaks everyone, but then some become strong in the broken places.*[100] Like Hemingway, the world broke Mark and tragically he was not among the *some*. To honor his memory, let us pray that God will enable us to become strong at this broken place in our lives. Let us *choose life* (Deuteronomy 30:15), as we call upon this wondrous God who can do *far more for us than we could ever ask or imagine* (Ephesians 3:20b).

---

[100] *The Enduring Hemingway* (New York: Chas Scribner, 1974), p. 322.

Memorial Service

Jill Challender Shelley

I first knew Jill through her picture. It was on the night I accepted the call to come to First Presbyterian, and I was looking through the activity pages in the church's pictorial directory. There she is, teaching a class of Haitian children, and everyone is holding up for approval what looks like the first fold in the beginnings of their own paper airplane. I recall being struck by the joy in her face and the enthusiasm of all those children with their little arms in the air. Something told me then, Jill was beautiful.

Now, I'm not speaking of her good looks that could and did light up every room she entered. If that weren't enough, her generous smile gave you the feel of a warm embrace on a chilly day. And if that couldn't get you, well then you were simply not available to be gotten!

The one she really wanted to get to of course, her devoted husband, Dick. If there was such a thing as an unending honeymoon, they had it. Jill's decision to be a travel agent provided a doorway to the world, taking their honeymoon on the road, early and often. The joys they shared in every facet of their lives provide a fountain of memories, for Dick, and for us all, to draw upon.

What is appropriate for us to consider is the way the light of Christ shown through Jill's life – a picture of her at the Siloe School in the mountains of the Cormier watershed in Haiti, is a perfect glimpse. That is, the qualities of Jill's inner beauty; those ways Christ was revealed in and through her. This inner beauty I speak of is what the saints of the church describe as the beauty of righteousness.

It was her heart for the things close to the divine heart that made her beauty so expansive and life-giving to us all. Hers was a heart for mission, a voice of praise in worship, an elder leading the church, a servant on humanitarian agencies like Religious Community Services, giving strength to the voice of the poor. Jill was very much one like Jesus who Luke tells us in his second book, *went about doing good* (Acts 10:34). In her it all seemed a pleasure and in her it all rang true.

If you notice, the fruit of the Spirit, Paul tells the Galatians is not *fruits* in the plural, but fruit in the singular.[101] Someone led by the Spirit is not one who gives evidence of merely one of these qualities, rather Paul is saying that one who is truly led by the Spirit gives evidence of them all. And Jill did. As we observed her in action, when she didn't know anyone was looking, we saw what that mature and ripened fruit of the Spirit looks like. She made the Christian life appear as it truly is: attractive, desirable, wise, the only way to live.

There is no getting away from the fact that her death seems so premature, so wasteful, so senseless. Who among us could fault Dick for taking to his lips the complaint of *King Lear* who exclaimed after the death of Cordelia, *Why should a dog, a horse, a rat, have life/And thou no breath at all?*[102] There is no satisfactory explanation that can fill the void created when bereft of one you love at any age, one you appreciate, admire, value, one who has nearly been the heart of your own heart. While Jesus' says, God *makes his sun rise on the evil and on the good and sends rain on the righteous and unrighteous* (Matthew 5:45) alike, may give us a

---

[101] Galatians 5:22-23

[102] William Shakespeare, *King Lear*, Act V, sc. III, Lines 363-4.

helpful perspective, it provides little consolation.

Because we are human, we want to know why; because we are only human, we cannot know why. What we need, is what we have. It is precisely by the faith that we share with Jill, that you and I can penetrate the veil of tragedy, disease and death, and touch something that is constant and true, that something or Someone, who is in and through, before and beyond this life, all of life. This is the power given us as Christians that is the difference between those who are crushed by circumstances and those who transcend them, or, as the medieval mystic Meister Eckhart put it, *transfigure* them. Had not the inexorable nature of this disease become so swift and debilitating at its hurried end, I believe Jill would have had the time and energy to share with us her experience of this as well. As the school of Christ continues all the way to the end, at her end, Jill continued her growth as a disciple.

No one need tell us that life even at its longest, is brief. Death is the fate humans share with all creation. But there is another kind of death to which the Christian is called that leads us to our destiny, it is a death that sets us apart from all else, and perhaps all others. The Apostle Paul told the Corinthians, *I die every day* (1 Corinthians 15:31). He is saying that this life we have in Christ is a daily experience of dying and rising with Christ. Every day we practice our final dying as we daily become dead to the temporary, the passing, the ephemeral, the fleshly and worldly desires and fears. And every day we practice our rising to that final dawn, as we daily become alive to the eternal, enduring, unending spiritual and heavenly hopes and loves, all in fact, that Jill is now enjoying.

This my friends is the faith that Jill found in Christ and lived so convincingly. As William Sloane Coffin said after the funeral of his own son, this is the faith that is *born in that love that never dies and is nourished in the peace and dazzling grace that always is.*[103]

---

[103] Tom Long and Cornelius Plantinga, ed. *A Chorus of Witnesses*, William Sloane Coffin, *Alex's Death"* (Eerdmans: Grand Rapids, 1994), p. 265

Memorial Service

Donald Frank Selover

Like every one of us is in our own way, Donald Frank Selover, was a contradiction. Baptized an Episcopalian in New York State, he lived most of his life as a Presbyterian in North Carolina, and a Sunday School Superintendent; as one who loved flying, and airplanes, who had himself studied aeronautics, piloted a plane; would spend his life's work with companies who made boats, *aquanautics* as he liked to call it.

Unlike far too few of us, Donald Frank Selover was consistent; he was a consistent and faithful man whose words to Susan at the last, *I love you* confirmed what she knew, what he showed her repeatedly through their years together. This love for his sister, father and mother was as palpable and real as they could have wanted.

Susan's daughter Lee Ann found in him her true father. *Like apples of gold in baskets of silver*, Donald's counsel to her was *fitly spoken* (Proverbs 25:11) she said, he always said the right word, always what she needed to hear, always at the right time. It is no surprise how easy Susan's family claimed him, *like our own son* said Susan's father, W.C. And their mutual regard and affection was transparent to all. A true friend in school, and colleague at work, his kindness and sense of fairness, was his way with everyone.

Around the time of his diagnosis, at his request for a modern Bible translation, I gave him Eugene Peterson's translation of *The Message*. I also shared with Donald a book I thought we might read together, as its author, Philip Simmons also had ALS – Lou Gehrig's disease. Simmons began writing it when he was first diagnosed at age 35. It chronicles his gradual bodily demise, while sharing the deeper meaning of life he was simultaneously awakening to. The book is entitled: *Learning to Fall*.

Donald, as everyone knew, was a man of few words. But alone with him, he did talk. On several occasions we would talk in my study, but mostly we talked over lunch at Hams and later over, take out I brought to the house, and sometimes when I just stopped by. We talked about Simmons' book and a lot of other things. But mostly we sat in silence. That was fine, silence is good. He did however find interesting one story – as a parable from Zen Buddhism that Donald said was their mutual predicament:

> *A certain man was crossing a field when he saw a tiger charge at him. The man ran, but the tiger gained on him, chasing him toward the edge of a cliff. When he reached the edge, the man had no choice but to leap. He had one chance to save himself from momentary death: a scrubby branch growing out of the side of the cliff about halfway down. He grabbed the branch and hung on. Looking down, what did he see on the ground below? Another tiger.*

He looked a few feet over to his left, and saw a small plant growing out of the cliff. And from it hung one ripe strawberry. Letting go with one hand, he was able to stretch his arm out just far enough to pluck the berry with his fingertips and bring it to his lips.

How sweet it tasted! [104]

---

[104] Philip Simmons, *Learning to Fall: The Blessings of an Imperfect Life* (Bantam Dell: New York, 2000), pp. 4-5.

Tigers either way, <u>that's it</u>, Donald emphasized.

Silence.

Have you looked around to see if there is a strawberry somewhere in reach? I asked. *It is hard to see anything from where I've been recently to where I am now.*

More silence.

Indeed, it must have been, I thought to myself, having as happened to Donald: laid off after 31 years by his company wanting to trim costs, a worrisome interim before securing more work, followed almost immediately by his horrific diagnosis, and then, as insult to injury, the machinations of social security eligibility moving at the pace of spilled molasses.

As our conversations continued, we would return to that parable. Though I did not know this, according to the family, Donald was famous for saying, *I'm going to have to think about that for a while.* Now I, realize how many times I heard him say that myself. He apparently thought about those tigers and that strawberry. And so, we sat in silence. For the longest time and understandably so, For the longest time, and understandably, he was consumed by those tigers; and God seemed absent. *It's hard not to think of all who I will miss*, he said.

For several visits our conversations went to other things; matters of faith and doubt, questions the prophet Job could have asked and would have certainly appreciated, and other matters of life and the life everlasting. But mostly it was silence.

Late last summer, early fall, he brought it up; he saw I had brought my copy of Simmons book. Eyeing it under my arm, he started, *I've had a hard time with that book because of its title,* he began *Learning to Fall.* I figured he was going to say he quit reading it, because I sensed he didn't like it, but no. He said, *What seemed the very opposite, now makes sense to me.*

What do you mean, I questioned?...*Falling.* .... *"Falling?"* I said.

He said, "*Falling is harder than climbing; we spend a lifetime climbing: growing up, school, work, making a living. We don't know how to fall; you've got to be knocked down to know what falling feels like. I've been knocked down...... but good ....*

Silence.

How many people really notice themselves dying? he said suddenly, *and yet this is everyone's future.*

Silence....

When you have no choice but accept it as I'm trying to do, you wish you had learned it earlier. Learning to fall may be the best way to know how to climb. Doesn't Jesus say something like that? Yes, he does. (Mark 8:35-36, par.)

Silence....

The things you notice about yourself and others, is amazing. *I think I'm falling upwards, into really being alive, now that my body is quitting on me, and I have no choices to make except those inside of me. I don't always feel this way; tomorrow I may be depressed again. But there is joy in me at times I've never felt, looking at the clouds in the sky. I can shut my eyes and imagine flying ...... God is good.*

That was the last real one-on-one conversation we had. There was one more thing I wanted to tell him, this one who appreciated Eagles' wings, the God of the Sparrow, so I'll tell you. In his book, *Night Flight*, the French World War II aviator, Antoine de St. Exupery, tells of an incident while flying that is kind of parable for our lives.

> *Once while flying over the Sahara at sunset I became hopelessly lost. As darkness fell I searched desperately for the light of the nearest airport. Suddenly on the horizon I saw a blinking light. With joy and relief, I turned my plane toward that light only to discover in minutes that I was headed toward a rising star. Then I turned toward another blinking light, confidently flying toward it, only to find in minutes that again, it was but another star. Time and again I frantically turned my plane toward a far-off light of hope and promise only to be disappointed. There I was [he wrote], lost in the vastness of the night, going from one light to another, desperately searching for that one that one light that could*
> *guide me safely home.*[105]

In thankfulness this day, we can trust Christ's promise, and believe Donald's Lord and ours, led him safely home.

---

[105] Antoine De Saint Exupery, *Night Flight* (Wilmington MA: Houghton Mifflin Harcourt, 1974).

Memorial Service
Nancy Louise Hagy Chiles

Every one of us is one of a kind, we say. Once born the mold is broken, we say. There can never be another one just like you, we say. This truism seems particularly true for Nancy Chiles. One example. Among the many hats she wore here at First Presbyterian, Nancy was our flower coordinator. Dutiful to a fault, to her it made no difference that she arranged flowers for her own husband's memorial service than that for any other members' loved ones. That was Nancy. I wouldn't put it past her pre-arranging the flowers for her own service today.

She was a Presbyterian Blue-blood from Big Stone Gap, Va., who mastered the Smaller Catechism when she was little more than a tyke. A graduate from her beloved William and Mary with a double major in Physics and English, she was hired by NASA fresh out of school to work on what would become all six of the Mercury Missions at Langley Field, from May 1961 to May 1963. This was the Cold War, and the Sputnik had to be answered.

But all work and no play was not her thing. According to her children she enjoyed in college, in her summers back in Big Stone Gap, and after hours in Hampton, Va. racing around in her MGA Roadster and then a Triumph, TR3. Much to her consternation a college boyfriend borrowed it and installed seat belts. When a tube of lipstick that was not hers rolled out from under her seat at a stop light, she told him, *This relationship is over, don't you think?* She then tore out the seatbelts.

After NASA came Bob and their move to New Bern to raise their family. It is hard to believe that thirteen months ago, we were here for Bob's service. Tomorrow is his birthday, and perhaps we can say that Nancy is his birthday present. Two lives lived well. Like Bob, she was heavily involved through the years in numerous service organizations and clubs, that worked for the good of our community. For any number of reasons, it is painful to think they are no longer here with us.

I met Nancy as a member of the Pulpit Nominating Committee, that came for me in the summer of 2000. It would take the committee more than a year to track down and speak to every person I have ever known. When I told Nancy she and the committee had overlooked my second-grade teacher, without missing a beat she said, *We tried; but she was dead.*

When, in time I learned Nancy was once a technical editor translating scientific gibberish into the vernacular mere mortals could understand, I knew she had to be a grammatical nightmare to those around her. Before I knew any of her children I immediately felt compassion for all three. Six months ago, in a moment of lapsed judgment on my part, I asked Nancy for her help on some writings I'm to have published. Well let me tell you, it was Mrs. McDonald's fourth grade class at Raleigh Court Elementary all over again. My first two-hour experience with Nancy left my eyes glazed over in a film of red ink. We stopped, for the day. As I left she said, *We did well, Bill. You didn't cuss at me once!* With the ball over the plate, low and inside, I couldn't resist, *Well, then, the hell with you!* I never saw her laugh as much.

Nancy once told my wife Lori, that *Bill and I share our tough mountain stock from southwestern, Virginia.* Well, I'm not so sure "tough" would describe me, but I have no doubt about her. She could be blunt and cocksure that was off-putting to those she had yet to break-in, and she couldn't help it that she was right far too often for her own good. But if you knew her you knew it was essential to her charm, if charm is what you'd call it!

She taught the Uniform Standard Lesson for her Sunday School Class, that according to her she'd been at *longer than Methuselah lived*. (For those of you who don't know, Methuselah is purportedly the oldest man in the Bible. He lived for 969 years.) Yes, Nancy had been at it for a long time – since at least the seventies – the year round, every year, the entire Bible every six years. Then she would begin again, and again, and over again.

Nancy talked theology with me many times, but most recently on the doctrine of predestination – which she fully embraced as a child. The version she learned in the Big Stone Gap Presbyterian Sunday School was the one taught by the Apostle Paul and St. Augustine. As she went through her life, she found it as the Bible intended it to be, a source of comfort and consolation, and never more so than with the end in sight.

Reading the Bible, she learned early on that history doesn't turn on a wheel like the cycle of nature. No, not a wheel forcing us to resign ourselves to the eternal return of the same, and with it, an indifferent fate. No, our lives are not governed by chance, luck, and fortune; the gods of this world capriciously doling out blessing and curse, bestowing good or evil upon whoever. Nancy knew that history is linear and moves from beginning to the middle to the end, and however much we are fated to die as befalls all of God's creatures, the faithful are to know they are living out a destiny. Regardless of circumstances we trust and live in the confidence that we are under the benevolent eye of the Lord our God, fulfilling a destiny that ends with God.

Not long before her death, Nancy said, *I was taught that we are to live as if it is 100% up to God, and act as if it was 100% up to you. So, I'm acknowledging God's 100% when I say this. I've done both till now,* and then she added, *there is not much left of my 100%.*

Our last visit was a week ago today, and it was over the phone. Out she came with this string of pearls: *I enjoy the story in Genesis 45 of Joseph and his brothers, when everything is out in the open and he tells them, "You meant evil for me, but God meant it for good." God overcomes our worst to make it the best,* she added. *I think of Psalm 139, "In your book were written all the days for me, when none of them yet existed. I like John 15 where Jesus said, "You didn't choose me, but I chose you". And Ephesians 1 where Paul says, "Blessed be the God and Father of our Lord Jesus Christ…..for choosing us in Christ before the foundation of the world….and then Romans 8, where he says, "All things work together for good for those who love God, who are called according to his purpose, predestined to be conformed to the image of his son; those he predestined he called, justified and glorified." She ended with the Second Letter to Timothy 1, citing the words, "I know the one in whom I have believed, and he is able to guard until that day what I have entrusted to him."*

That was the last thing I heard her say. It was enough.

Reckoning with Grief
2 Samuel 18:24-33; Psalm 77:1-14

I once had a philosophy professor who delighted in poking fun at religious faith – any faith – he was an equal opportunity despiser of them all. One day he questioned why Christians are upset at funerals; why they are weeping and not rejoicing in the resurrection? Though an immature sophomore, my professor's unwillingness to acknowledge those tears are for ourselves and not for the deceased, struck me as odd. Our grieving is in self-pity; it is a cry of absence, of being deprived of a loved one or friend, particularly one whose faith in God made more real and strengthened our own.

The text is from John's Gospel, describing Jesus' reaction to Lazarus' death. John says he was, *deeply moved* he *wept* and those who looked on said: *See how he loved him*. Whatever else about the situation prompted Jesus' anguish, his response gives us permission to weep openly rather than to try to deny and bottle up our emotions.

Some time ago after the husband of an elderly couple passed away, I was by to see his widow a month or so after the service. Like her husband, they had both lived an exemplary Christian life. Yet, as she told me, she had prayed hard to accept her husband's death as a Christian. She said that despite her efforts she couldn't control her tears and felt guilty for what she called, her *lack of faith*. That she believed her tears evidence of being faithless, nearly broke my heart. Jesus' example ought to tell us that nothing could be further from the truth. Just because a loved one's heart stops beating, it doesn't mean your heart stops loving. Our hearts are not emotional faucets we can turn on and off with a flick of the wrist. Those who love much, suffer much. You and I see it in Christ's love for all humanity on the Cross, and we discover it in ourselves when we lose someone near and dear to us. Referring to a dear friend who had died, St. Augustine wrote *My soul and that of my friend had been one soul in two bodies. So, I had a horror of going on living because I did not wish to live on as half a person.*[106] He speaks for many of us. And so, the pain of grief is in greater measure trying to let go of a large part of who you are that died with him.[107]

The mistaken impression that Christian faith forbids grieving is compounded by a society marginally acquainted with suffering and death, by its preoccupation with any and every means of denial, particularly with our obsession of looking youthful. It takes at least two to four years to grieve a loved one's death, but our society gives you about six weeks to get over it.[108] Then comes the not-so-subtle message – to put on a cheery face or else something must be wrong with you. So, if you are only four years out from some great personal loss and are still feeling it, you are normal so do not let anyone tell you otherwise.

This is especially true, when nature's order has been reversed and it is your child or grandchild whose death you mourn, just as David's poignant desire to have died in place of his son Absalom. If there are certain life experiences that require patience, grieving is one of them. Impatience is a learned defect we've absorbed from our culture, that is why we are almost always dealing with residual, unresolved grief. There is in all of us some grief yet to be addressed that sometimes underlies

---

[106] Augustine, *Confessions*, Book IV, 6.

[107] Henri Nouwen, *In Memoriam* (Notre Dame: Ava Maria Press, 1980), p. 37.

[108] Bryant Kirkland, *A Pattern For Faith*, (Fifth Avenue Presbyterian Church, 1983), p. 181.

emotional reactions we cannot explain. If you want evidence that residual grief exists, simply attend movies or plays in which the plot evokes strong emotions of love and loss. There you are free to weep and not have to explain yourself. Powerful drama strikes a chord deep within, exposing lingering, residual grief. It is not for those on the stage or in the movie we weep, but the painful, even the awe-inspiring moments triggered in our psyche, most we cannot begin to identify.

Grief is a natural emotion that comes with any loss, not just that of a loved one: from divorce to an amputation; to leaving your neighborhood to move to another state; of learning of the death of an old friend you haven't seen or heard from in years but you had a history before and it matters now; for veterans in all military branches who have fought in our nations war and conflicts, who came home when compatriots they relied on for their life did not, even when turning the pages of the calendar and the awareness sinks in, of days no longer to be lived, only remembered, if that. Missed opportunities or days of glory, are both alike now. To realize that was then; this is now, means loss. A moment of truth comes to you, when you discover that losing is living. The impatient youth who cannot wait to grow up looks back years later and wonders what the hurry was.

Though I'm primarily addressing times of death, grief is a reality of living at any time. In any case, these occasions can be opportunities of growth or ruin. Life is a series of choices, and as one sage put it, *not to decide is to decide.* What I want for all of us, is to consciously, deliberately and faithfully pray our way to our help in time of need.

Shock, grief and rebuilding, are three broad strokes that outline the experience: from discovery or realization of loss, to acceptance, and charting a new course living again. The way grief is experienced is unique to the circumstances and the person you are. There are some losses that occur years before an actual death. The relief that comes after the death of one who has suffered little or no quality of life for some length of time is nothing to be ashamed about. The *loss* happened a long time ago, at no one identifiable moment, but gradually by way of an accumulation of many moments. Even acknowledging the relief is as much for them as you, it is normal to experience a mixture of contradictory emotions.

My concern is that when we experience grief that we respond to it in a way appropriate as Christians. And to realize, whether religious or not, how pent-up grief has a way of taking itself out on our bodies, just as stress is known to cause heart problems and stomach ulcers. The subconscious motives that provoke bodily symptoms and unhealthy responses in our behavior and relationships we call "psychosomatic," were well known to our Hebrew ancestors, but only recently appreciated anew, in the last hundred years of medicine.

I'm going to offer three suggestions I believe of a biblically informed way to handle your grief.

First – You need to build a life worthy of grief. As a Christian, your life is to be anchored in your devotion to God. Your devotion is actualized as you increase in your desire to grow in Christ's Spirit, and that his very life, will ripen and flourish in you. Don't look at Christians: look at Jesus whom you see and hear in the Gospel accounts. Through Scripture, personal prayer, corporate worship, witnessing by all you are and have, you discover *what life is all about* as the saying goes.

Your life is an opportunity to sanctify the life of others by the Christ they find in you. And if you consider persons now deceased, who loom largest in your heart and mind – besides relatives and those most immediate in your extended family – that those in your deepest affections and thoughtful recollections, are they not the ones who were most Christ-like; not the wealthiest, most athletic, the smartest, the best-looking, none of these? Is it not the ones who sacrificed, whose living was in the giving, whose life's focus held a different orientation – a life centered in God. It was about such persons that author and composer John Bell wrote: *Though unacclaimed by earthly powers, your life through theirs has hallowed ours.*[109]

The early church called the making of a life – *Ars Moriendi* – *the art of dying*, to have a *good death*.[110] Early Christians believed dying to be an art or craft, developed over the course of life. To die artfully, to have a *good death*, it is necessary to have a good life, that is, one lived faithfully.

Immediately after his wife's death, social critic Studs Terkel who was then 89 years-old and in what proved to be his last book wrote *Will the Circle Be Unbroken*.[111] In an interview with Charlie Rose he said that though he intended to write a book about the deaths of those he admired, he could only find words of instruction about how to live. Terkel unwittingly expressed the forgotten wisdom of the early church saying, *These people died well, because they lived well.*

---

[109] John Bell, *The Last Journey*, Iona Community: Gia Publishing, 1996, p. 37.

[110] Another meaning of the Latin, Ars Moriendi or "good death," is the English word of Greek origin: *euthanasia*.

[111] Terkel, *Will the Circle Be Unbroken: Reflections on Death, Rebirth, and A Hunger for Faith* (New York: Ballantine Readers Circle, 2002).

Second – Rely on God's faithfulness. I say this because you can be honest with God in a way only God can hear and respond. You can level with God in a way no individual can hear. What your family of faith and friends offer is invaluable and needed. What God offers is uniquely God's to give.

One of the best places to look is in the Book of Psalms. In his commentary, John Calvin says the Psalms possess *an anatomy of all parts of the soul; for no one will find in himself a single feeling of which the image is not reflected in the mirror.*[112] Calvin's observations are never more true than in times of loss, fear, grief and feelings of abandonment. Consider Jesus' words on the Cross:

> *My God, my God, why have you forsaken me… so far from helping me …. I cry to you by day, but you do not answer; and by night and I find no rest.* (Psalm 22:1-2)

And yet, it is this same psalmist who writes that God can turn *our mourning into dancing* (30:11). The Psalms of Lament for individuals and communities of faith, follow a pattern that take us through grief, anguish and peril, yet emerge with restored confidence in God's sovereign care. In our own adversities, we can take our confidence in the ultimate outcome. Even when your own faith is failing, you can borrow on theirs. For it is the Psalm in its entirety, that it's intention and meaning are found. Even if, it is hard medicine to swallow, read it, to the end. It is at the end we find the final truth expressed by Julian of Norwich, *All shall be well, and all shall be well, and all manner of things shall be well.*[113]

---

[112] James Mays, *The Lord Reigns*, (Louisville: W/JKP, 1994), p. 46.

[113] Julian of Norwich, *The Classics of Western Spirituality: Showings* (Mahwah: NJ, Paulist Press, 1978).

Third – Expect God's Spirit to lead you into greater spiritual maturity. I realize some of our older members might smile at the idea of *greater maturity*. But it is true. Just as you never stop growing and maturing spiritually, the Spirit of God seeks to unite more deeply with your spirit throughout your life – and in times of mourning, perhaps you are the most open to God's will for you.

The disciples of Jesus mourned for 40 days, trying to comprehend what had happened. In this long period of mourning the spirit was working in and upon and even through them, preparing them to receive the Spirit. As Jesus said in his farewell discourses:

> *It is to your advantage that I go away, for if I do not go away, the Advocate (Spirit) will not come to you; but if I go, I will send him to you. When the Spirit of truth comes, he will guide you into all the truth…* (John 16: 7, 13a)

When grieving the loss of loved ones, there is more to it than many realize. The Spirit's intention for your present and future is at stake. Through the deaths of others, the Spirit is giving you yet another opportunity to learn more of the truth about yourself, about God, about your ultimate destiny.[114] These things may be among those Jesus said you could not bear to hear, that will be said. The question then will be whether you have the faith and courage to hear (John 16:12).

It is then that the deceased for whom you grieve becomes a participant in God's ongoing work of redemption. In and through the Spirit of Christ, your loved ones who have beaten you to grave are even now transformed as a new part of who

---

[113] Henri Nouwen, *In Memoriam* (Notre Dame: Ava Maria Press, 1980), p. 37.

you are and are yet becoming.

Living a life worthy of grief, looking to God's consolations in Scripture, and expecting the Spirit to deepen and renew you for what is still to come, is the way of God's healing and renewing strength.

How to Help Others Handle Their Grief

1 Kings 17:17-24; Luke 7:11-17

Many years ago, a publisher told me *If you want to get something published, write a How to Book*. Though Dale Carnegie's vintage *How to Win Friends and Influence People* came immediately to mind, I could not think of any modern examples. *What do you have in mind?* Something, like *How to Succeed in Business Without Really Trying, How to Raise Children at Home in Your Spare Time*, or *How to Become a Bishop without Being Religious*.

This summer however you will be hearing some *How to* sermons. I do this with some trepidation. Matters of the Christian life cannot be reduced to a checklist of do's and don'ts. But, I forge ahead because I also know that behaving like a Christian can be the path of discovery that awakens a person to their heart's desire. Along the path your dutiful beginning may lead to your desire to continue, the experience has been transformed into a *habit of the heart*. Your path of devotion to Christ takes you down more adventurous avenues of faith, the expression of which takes on flesh and blood service with one's neighbor.

When Paul tells the Church at Galatia that we are to *bear one another's burdens*, he certainly includes caring for those burdened by grief. And what burden is greater, or the one we are most called upon to share, than to help one another in times of grief?

In today's Scripture texts, Elijah and Jesus are seeking to comfort widows who have lost their only son. Both stories conclude with their sons' miraculous resuscitation.

Commentators agree that the emphasis of these accounts is indirectly a display of God's miraculous power, and primarily our Lord's compassion for these distraught widows.

It is claimed that genuine compassion, free of self-interest, does not come naturally. In his book, *Giving and Taking Help*, psychologist, Alan Keith-Lucas writes, *All helping has a religious base and the desire to help another person is not, as far as we know, from instinct.*[115] Whether recognized or not, it is God's Spirit of Christ that prompts our caring. And as Christians, we depend on the Holy Spirit's guiding and empowering presence to truly be of help, so to faithfully and wisely care for another. Henri Nouwen says, *Sorrow is an unwelcome companion and anyone who willingly enters into another's pain is truly a remarkable person.*[116]

Many of us draw back excusing ourselves by not knowing what to say or do. To be of use in helping another bear such a burden, you don't begin wondering what to say or do. You are much better off to begin by considering, who you are and what you have to give. Who you are and what you have to give, is *you!* That's it. The good news is, it is enough, in fact, it is just right.

The problems begin when you try to be someone you are not. There are almost always others in the constellation of support whose role you are not to assume. What is more, there are certain things only God can do for this burdened soul and certain things only they can do for themselves. Being who you are is enough. If someone needs you, it is you they need not by your being nervous and uptight, trying to be someone you are

---

[115] Alan-Keith Lucas, *Giving and Taking Help* (Chapel Hill: UNC Press, 1972), p. 200.

[116] Henri Nouwen, *In Memoriam*, p. 14

not. And do not be surprised by laughter for often they are the same emotional release.

John Westerhoff tells of a Catholic priest who visited a couple in his congregation whose child had just died. The priest was a close friend and could only cry with them in their living room the day the news broke. Embarrassed at having been of so little use to them, he was surprised when a week after the funeral, the mother greeted him back into their home saying *We are so glad you've come again. We wanted to thank you for all you did for us.* Puzzled, the priest said, *But I didn't do anything but sit with you and cry.* And she said, *But you gave us yourself, and that was what we needed.*[117]

If being yourself is of first importance then secondly, know that you need not to have experienced what the grieving person is going through to be of help. Certainly, there is benefit in talking with persons in like circumstances, as support groups of various kinds have proved invaluable. But you need not to have endured a similar loss, to be of help. In some case, a common experience can be a liability.

When as chaplain at the Medical College of Virginia, one day I was sitting with a woman whose husband had been dead less than an hour. Minutes after my arrival a friend of hers whose husband had died less than two years before, arrived. She talked non-stop for a half an hour, describing everything she knew her friend was now going through. Dealing as she was with her own grief, she was far too preoccupied with herself to be present for her now grieving friend. My point being, you do not need to have experienced a common loss to share a friend's

---

[117] John Westerhoff, *Will Our Children Have Faith* (Minneapolis: Winston Press, 1990), p. 10.

burden. Elijah and Jesus did not have to lose sons to comfort these mothers. Nor do any of us.

In the third place, you are to be present and listen. You need not say anything. Nor for that matter, does he or she. Silence is O.K. and you need hear that silence is O.K. and trust it. *Be still and know that I am God* (Psalm 46:10) writes the psalmist.

The Spirit seems to prefer a silent listening to be heard. I want to emphasize the value of silence because merely sitting alone in silence much less with someone else, has become a serious problem for our generation. Most cannot stand it and want only to remedy the silence by filling the air with noise. There used to be such a thing as an *awkward* silence. These days, when speaking of silence, *awkward* has become redundant. It is as though *every* silence is awkward and needs to be broken. In your anxiety of wanting to break the silence while believing you need to say something helpful, you only become absent for that person. Quit worrying about the silence or obsessing over what to say. Trust the silence. Trust Jesus' counsel. On one occasion Jesus advised the disciples saying, *do not worry beforehand what you are to say; but say whatever is given you at that time…*(Mark 13:11). Or consider that the Holy Spirit gives you nothing to say, because silence is what you are given to share. An old saying that needs reclaiming: *Silence is golden.*

Let me also say that there are no *right words* so don't grope for them. Overused worn out slogans and hackneyed phrases are just noisy chatter that everyone, including the person grieving has heard many times. However, much you want to say something helpful, I assure you, that burdened soul is not waiting with baited breath for great pearls of wisdom to fall from your lips. You remember Job's friends were doing just fine caring for him until they opened their mouths. While there are no *right words* to say, they demonstrate that there are lot of things you should never say.

At a conference on grieving, Pastors Suzanne Schultz and Jane Harmes, whose husbands died of terminal diseases, shared a list of things they believe should never be said. The two women did their own top ten countdown of things said to them, that should *never ever* be said to someone after a loved one has died:

10. God needs him more than you do.
9. God gave him this disease in order to test you.
8. God never gives you more than you can handle.
7. God needs another angel and has come for him ahead of time.
6. I know exactly how you feel. My cat (or even my husband) died last week.
5. I'm sorry this is so bad for you because I love you and this is terribly hard on me.
4. Well, you wouldn't want him to live in the shape he's in, would you?
3. According to Kubler-Ross, the next stage after shock is anger... are you angry yet?
2. You think this is bad, you wouldn't believe what once happened to my uncle, all in the same week.
1. So, when your husband dies, do you think you'll remarry?[118]

While the last six of these mentioned are too trite to address, the first four are examples of persons who have taken over God's role. Whatever eternal validity there is in paraphrasing or saying, *God doesn't put on us anymore than we can bear* (1

---

[118] *Monday Morning*, Vol. 59/3, Feb 7, 1994, (I've added, #3 and #9 from personal experience).

Corinthians 10:13) or *God works together for good* (Romans 8:28a) either or like sayings,[119] spoken to a grieving person is simply cruel, and in the circumstances, equivalent to a lie.

Following the death of his wife Joy, C.S. Lewis wrote a diary later published in book form, entitled *A Grief Observed*. Immediately after her death, he makes the following entry:

> *Talk to me about the truth of Christianity and I'll listen gladly. Talk to me about the duty of Christianity and I'll listen submissively. But don't come talking to me right now about the consolations of Christianity or I shall suspect you don't understand.*[120]

Lewis would never say that conversations about faith and God's promises do not have a place, only not the first thing to say. Even if the grieving soul raises it, you cannot respond on a cognitive level, but only a feeling one. My belief such faith affirmations are only appropriately said by the one grieving, not often heard till much later, and then as testimony to his or her experience.

I've often been suspicious that a lot religious talk is a cover to hide behind for a would-be comforter, to avoid entering the grief of the one who suffers. As it protects one too frightened to be truly present, their pious prattle further injures the grieving by making them feel guilty for their *unfaithfulness* for their grief. Sorrow truly is an unwelcome *companion*. Consequently, we live in a society more inclined to ignore our grief or help you hide or silence it with the offer of a sedative, or encouragement to take a vacation than, to simply be present

---

[119] Proverbs 3:11; Hebrews 2:18, 12:5-6; Revelation 3:19

[120] C.S. Lewis, *A Grief Observed* (London: Faber & Faber, 1961), p. 28.

a faithful witness, sharing a friend's burden if only in silence. It takes courage to go to someone in their grief and be vulnerable to another in their anguish.

And fourthly, and finally, remember. Last week, I said grief takes two to four years at a minimum. Don't be a part of that public that gives a grieving person six weeks and in effect says, *get over it*. As it takes time and patience, so are your sympathies timely and patiently to go the distance with them. A month after the flurry of visits at the house, several months after the service and reception, the returned casserole dishes and notes of thanks, comes the reality of absence that has only just begun to weigh the longest and heaviest. When it is over for almost everyone else, it has just begun for the one grieving. We sing, *Blest be the Tie that Binds*. Let me say that blessed is the person who continues to pray for, visit, and talks to, another about their well-being, when others have forgotten.

In that remembering, speak of the deceased, for however gone from sight, the one loved and lost is present in the memories of those who grieve. This may seem like rubbing salt in the wound, but it is one of, if not the most helpful of ways to help another grieve. You might be surprised how eagerly the grieving person wants to remember out loud with someone. As one widow wrote about her grief, she said:

> *Why don't they talk about my husband? Every time I enter the room they become quiet. I yearn for someone to say his name, for someone to say, "Remember the time we went to the World's Fair together"....to remember things. But a wall drops as soon as the conversation nears saying something about him.*[121]

---

[121] Bryant Kirkland, *A Pattern For Faith*, (New York: Fifth Avenue Presbyterian Church, 1983), pp. 181-182.

It is one thing to live in the past, it is quite another to try and close off the nurturing, life-giving memories that shaped the lives we have in the present. Be for your friend a safe presence to hear and share those memories. Listening as she or he remembers, is key.

Being yourself, knowing of your ability to help without having to have had a similar loss, being present and listening, and sharing the ongoing patience of the one grieving, remembering with them, the one loved and lost, but only for a time.

This is a way of bearing another's burdens. The Spirit of Christ at work within you and me, enabling us to be a Christ to others as they grieve. Let us thank God, for allowing us to be a gift to others. Amen.

www.ingramcontent.com/pod-product-compliance
Lightning Source LLC
Chambersburg PA
CBHW070614010526
44118CB00012B/1513